Maybe it was the beauty of the place, or the marketing power of the words "Made in Vermont" that attracted the ten couples profiled in this book to set up our family-run food businesses in this state, but there's certainly a mystique about the "Green Mountains" that has been a magnet as much for entrepreneurs as it has been for skiers and nature lovers. I extol the virtues of Vermont at the risk that thousands of readers across the country will pull up stakes and join the throngs seeking fame, fortune and sanity out of the rat race.

But this book isn't meant to be an advertisement for Vermont, nor is it just about the food business. I think that our stories, and the lessons we've learned over the years, are universal. I'd venture to say that in our combined experiences you'll find just about every variation, permutation, challenge and triumph one is likely to experience in any entrepreneurial endeavor. None of us were experts in our respective businesses when we started. Most of us had more chutzpah than common sense. But we survived and we hope that our tales of the trials and tribulations of running a business with your significant other will inspire—and caution—dreamers everywhere.

"Uncle Dave" Lyon

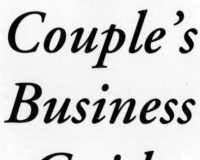

The

Couple's Business Guide

How to Start and Grow a
Small Business Together

Amy Lyon

A Perigee Book

A Perigee Book
Published by The Berkley Publishing Group
200 Madison Avenue
New York, NY 10016

First edition: May 1997

Published simultaneously in Canada.

The Putnam Berkley World Wide Web site address is
http://www.berkley.com

Library of Congress Cataloging-in-Publication Data

Lyon, Amy.
    The couple's business guide : how to start and grow a small
business together / Amy Lyon. — 1st ed.
        p.   cm.
    ISBN 0-399-52300-6
    1. Couple-owned business enterprises — Vermont — Case
studies. 2. New   business   enterprises — Vermont — Case
studies. I. Title.
HD62.27.L96   1997
658'.02'2 — DC20   96-46205
                                                            CIP
                                                            Rev.

Printed in the United States of America

10 9 8 7 6 5 4 3 2 1

To my son, Max.
Follow your dreams.

Acknowledgments

Who didn't help me? That list would be shorter. I am indebted to so many people for their support and encouragement.

Early on Nan Chesser and Ellen Cohen believed in me when I didn't believe in myself. Thank you to Cynthia Whitehouse, Mary Jane Eustace, Beryl Salinger Schmitt, Julia Starzyk, Claire Day and Mitzi Mackler for reading draft after draft. Ken Whitehouse for his technological assistance. Ken White for the opportunity to write for his paper (giving me the courage to go forward). Margaret Lobenstein for herself. Barbara Camp for her writing group, living room, and ultimately her home; and for first telling me that I would write a book. Howard Rosenthal for his encouragement at the beginning of this project. Stephen Krevalin for his legal advice. Diane Balestri who fed me. Joe Balestri who paid me and the entire staff at Caffeine's for listening to me. Tovia Smith for teaching me early on about the "rewrite." My entire writing group, Longmeadow Writers and Poets, who propped me up more than once. To David Saffer for being a good friend. To my whole family, notably Mom, J.B., and Cynnie for listening to me and encouraging me. Harriet Samol for her ready ear, day and night, and whose words are worth much more than gold.

Simply, without Beth Clifford, this book would not exist.

To my dad and Lynne for giving me this opportunity. I love you. And Ed Gildae who helped us all.

Finally, thanks to all the couples who not only welcomed me into their lives and businesses but also sent me home with good things to eat.

Contents

3: Getting the Business Started

4: Who's Running the Business?

5: Your Employees Are Your Business

6: When to Get Help

7: Sales and Marketing

8: To Grow or Hold the Line

9: Business as a Way of Life

The Couple's Business Guide

Introduction

Couples in business together: Some are like oil and water, and others are like two peas in a pod. Some scream at each other to communicate, then there are those who never seem to disagree. It doesn't matter what the mixture of traits and personalities is; what matters is what the couple does with the combination.

This is not a book about how to write a business plan, hire employees, or set up operating systems, although the importance of these and many other subjects is touched upon. There are many excellent books about any particular aspect of starting and running a business.

This book strives to give you a sense of what it will feel like to be in business with your spouse. You will meet ten couples in the gourmet food industry in Vermont. You will read about their passion and drive, their lessons learned and battles lost. Their stories are case studies of ten real businesses run by real couples in the real marketplace. There is next to nothing that these couples haven't experienced with the ups and downs of running a small business.

Their stories illuminate the stages of starting and running a business together—with all the inherent foibles and glory. Whether a business is opened by an individual, partners, or a married couple, the process of creating, running, and maintaining a business has the same components. First there is the dream fueled by passion. Then comes the period of research and planning; to find the right product and location, organize the structure of the business, write a business plan, raise capital, hire employees, devise a marketing strategy, produce the product, and the day-to-day job of running a business in order to meet the demands of the bottom line. To grow a business one needs to increase staff, learn how to delegate, and often take on more financial obligations. Ultimately a business is always in a stage of change and needs to be able to adapt in order to grow and be successful.

Coupledom brings to business a unique dynamic that affects the way the enterprise runs. The couple brings to the task twice the amount of skill and energy. A couple who decides to open a business is extending a personal dream of building a life and family in the marketplace. Their work life becomes an intregal part of their relationship, and their relationship shapes the business. They are a team that combines talents and strengths for the good of the business, their personal lives, and the community.

Business gives to a couple a new arena in which to grow where they become even closer to each other if only due to the sheer amount of time they spend together. This can prove challenging, although it is always illuminating. Often they become more balanced—roles are traded, and gender bias tends to diminish.

But the road through starting and running a business is

fraught with difficulty. For all the couples who have made it, there are many more who do not. A decision like this deserves much thought; the ramifications are great.

Nothing teaches better than experience. These couples offer you theirs to help you while you're creating your own.

1

The Dream

So You Want to Open
Your Own Business

"Honey, I have a great idea. Your blueberry spice jam is so good, we should package it! I know ten stores I could sell it to tomorrow."

How many times has someone uttered a statement like this while eating some delicious concoction?

What happens to those great ideas couples have? What becomes of their dream of opening a business together? How does a couple decide to go into business? What product to sell? Where to open it? When?

The advice you'll hear most often, and certainly throughout this book, is: not until after lots and lots of consideration, investigation, and a good long visit to your local shrink.

"Let's give it a try. We never see each other now. We can be our own bosses. We can make the decisions. No one will tell us what to do. We've always wanted to do something together."

This same couple talked lovingly about having their first baby: someone to carry on their name. Bring them joy in old age. A soft, pink smiling infant to hold and care for. But the reality can be shocking—a crying, colicky baby, sleep deprivation, ten or twenty extra pounds. And the ultimate realization . . . that this newborn will never go away. Think of your business as if you had just given birth to triplets—with no extra money for help.

There are those who can cook and make tastes come alive on the tongue, and then there are the rest of us, who might be better off turning our kitchen into a spare bedroom. Luckily for the husband/wife teams you will meet in this book, there are lots of us who would much rather buy than bake.

Why These Ten Couples Went into Business

Each one of these ten couples had their own reasons to start their own business. Davis and Ellen Koier of *Ward's Pond Farm* were tired of the particular demands of their full-time teaching jobs. They dreaded their locked-in schedule and lack of time together. Davis has a deteriorating eye condition which would soon have made it impossible to continue in his then-current position. They were already working together on weekends and during their summer vacations raising and selling organic produce and cut flowers at farmers' markets.

Having grown up on dairy farms, where the workday can be sixteen hours, seven days a week, with no differentiation between work and play, provided fertile training ground for Eric and Francine Chittenden of *Cold Hollow Cider Mill*. When, in the early years of their marriage, their own farming efforts proved unsuccessful, someone offered them an old cider press. That began their business, and now they have a landmark store in Waterbury, Vermont.

After many late-night talks and years of market research, Jonathan and Fran Rutstein were ready to return to their home state of Vermont and open a business. They bought a small business, *Bread & Chocolate*, that they found advertised in a Vermont newspaper. The price was right, so they jumped in. The first thing they learned was that only six of the six hundred accounts they had bought were active.

Diane and Richard Copley of *The Herb Patch* wanted out of the fast lane. They bought an existing business that was advertised in the *New York Times*. Their story is a cautionary tale—be sure you know what you are buying.

Sherrie Maurer was born and raised in the projects of inner-city Indianapolis. She and her husband, Hugh Maurer, created *Jasmine & Bread* after Sherrie was passed over for a promotion and won a discrimination suit. Frustration and the desire to prove herself propelled Sherrie, with Hugh, into business. She has successfully applied her street smarts to running a business.

Carol Berry and Jonathan Altman of *Putney Pasta* went to Vermont in the late seventies and didn't want to leave. Berry had experience in the hotel and restaurant industry, while Altman had run a contract food service company that catered to rock concerts. When their parents began to pressure them to move back to civilization, they brainstormed an idea—to open a vegetarian pasta company.

Jim MacIsaac started *Highland Sugarworks* by tapping the maple trees on his family's farm. Judy sweetened the company when she married him, and now they are one of the largest distributors of maple syrup in Vermont.

When Jacki Baker moved to Manchester, Vermont, from Rhode Island, she discovered *Mother Myrick's,* met the fudge maker Ron Mancini, and fell in love with the business and the baker. She eventually bought out Ron's previous boss; now she's the boss and has been for almost twenty years.

Uncle Dave's Kitchen was birthed by Lynne Andreen and her stepson J. B. Lyon. J.B., out of work as a staff member when Governor Michael Dukakis lost his presidential bid in 1988, asked Lynne if she could make an all-natural gourmet ketchup. They cooked up a business and subsequently invited J.B.'s father and Lynne's husband, Dave, aboard. Thus began a family affair.

Marilyn Wedig and Harry Haff, meeting in midlife, created *Yesterday's Kitchen* for their new life together. Harry had previous entrepreneurial experience, having owned and operated a bakery for five years, and Marilyn had spent years in the corporate world. They brought to the union different and complementary skills.

Desire, life's circumstances, unemployment, frustration, change of lifestyle, and health all played a role in propelling these couples into business. Some married into the business; others created their businesses together. One couple found the answer while fishing.

Ward's Pond Farm—The Facts

E llen (thirty-seven) and Davis (forty-nine) Koier made their first batch of smoked almonds for commercial sale in 1987. Their maple roasted, apple wood smoked almonds sold quickly at the farmers' markets and craft fairs where they had previously sold organic vegetables. They had found the product that would enable them to turn their seasonal business into a year-round enterprise. In 1989 Davis quit his teaching job to work full-time at Ward's Pond Farm. Ellen still teaches.

They were initially financed by personal savings and a $4,500 bank loan. Their sales for the first year were $13,000. In 1991 they incorporated their business and sold a percentage of their stock holdings to their lawyer, friend, and trusted advisor, Greg Clayton. Today, they work with a secured line of credit from the Union Bank of Morrisville, in Morrisville, Vermont, where they live and have their business.

The Koiers expanded their product line to include a variety of smoked and roasted nuts, plus Smokehouse Onions, Smokehouse Garlic, and Vermont maple syrup. Selling at shows and by mail order to a list of more than 17,000 names, Davis reports that Ward's Pond Farm sales in 1995 were over $200,000.

Davis and Ellen Koier with children, Davis Jr. and Abby

Davis and Ellen fished up a good one

On a hot summer afternoon in 1987, Ellen and Davis took a break from transplanting the rows of basil they were growing to sell at the farmers' market in Montpelier, Vermont. They loaded their canoe and fishing poles onto the back of their truck, stopped at a local market to pick up some worms, drinks, and snacks, and headed to Pulpit Rock to fish. They hoped to catch and later smoke some trout in a borrowed smoker. But the sky was a deep blue, the air was still, and the fish weren't biting. They leaned back, popped open a couple of cans of beer, and munched on smoked almonds.

With nothing else to do, they read the ingredients on the almond jar and were surprised by the amount of salt in the nuts and the fact that the smoked flavor was chemically produced. Davis started to speculate about whether an almond could be naturally smoked. What kind of wood would you use? What moisture would be needed? At what temperature would you roast and smoke a nut?

It wasn't trout that they smoked when arriving home that evening; it was almonds.

After many roastings and smokings, encouraged by their friends' opinions that they had indeed roasted the perfect confection, Ellen and Davis presented their first four-ounce cellophane bag of apple-wood-smoked almonds that fall at the farmers' market. They sold over 1,300 bags and grossed $2,000. They were on their way.

Eric and Francine Chittenden

Cold Hollow Cider Mill—The Facts

Francine (forty-four) and Eric (fifty-three) Chittenden have been running Cold Hollow Cider Mill since 1974. What started as a modest enterprise—custom grinding apples into cider for neighbors as well as producing their own cider to sell—has evolved into a $2,500,000 retail, wholesale, and mail-order business.

The Chittenden name goes back seven generations in Vermont, when Thomas Chittenden, Eric's ancestor, was the first governor of Vermont. Francine is a relative newcomer to the state, who moved there with her family when she was four years old.

Eric was (and still is) a merchant mariner. For the first fifteen years of their business he would be away at sea at least six months of the year while Francine ran the business and looked after their three children. It was his salary that kept the family afloat.

In 1976 Eric and Francine moved their business. Basing their purchase on highway density studies and traffic counts, they bought a home and barn on Route 100 in Waterbury Center, where they still live and work today. Within two months of purchase they moved into the house and opened their doors selling apple cider, maple syrup, and rocking horses. Today their store comprises a series of connected buildings that house a cider press, cider jelly house, retail store, mail-order operation, and bakery. The retail *sales make up 50 percent of their business, wholesale 33 percent, and mail order 17 percent.*

More than 650 tourist buses stop at Cold Hollow Cider Mill annually, which employs between twenty-five and fifty people, depending on the season. The mill sells one million gallons of fresh cider yearly.

He dreams them up, she makes them work

For Eric and Francine Chittenden, it was a series of trial-and-error experiments before they hit on the right venture and began their cider business. In 1972 Eric had purchased a 350-acre farm in Bakersfield, Vermont. He was living in a sugar house with no electricity when he wasn't away at sea. Once he and Francine married, he began to search for a way to make money as a land-lubber.

Although the farm had come with a herd of cows, it didn't take these two dairy kids long to realize that they weren't going to milk cows for the rest of their lives: two weeks, to be exact.

Eric needed no persuasion. After considering selling firewood (he tossed that idea out after cutting up enough wood for his own house), tapping maple syrup ("lots of glory, not much money," Eric said), and growing wheat ("never even planted because of the flood of '72," Francine remembered), they found their future in an abandoned cider press.

If Eric is the idea man in this couple, then it's Francine who can claim the title champion of the follow-up. For most of their married and business lives Eric would be away for months. Francine, in the age-old tradition of a sailor's wife, would run the house, tend the children, and in their case, run the ever expanding business of Cold Hollow Cider Mill.

"For many years Eric would be gone four to six months and come home just long enough to jolt the business into another massive growth spurt," Francine said. "Like the time he decided to open a restaurant in the adjoining building. We ran that for ten years."

Are You Ready to Dive In?

The Koiers and the Chittendens created their businesses in order to live where they wanted to and how they wanted to. They are living their dream by finding ways to turn ideas into action.

Are you ready to dive in? Do you want to test your skills? Do you have the stamina and energy? Are you ready to risk the known for the unknown? Dreaming is one thing; living a dream is quite another.

Turning a dream into reality takes planning, money, luck, and hard work. It doesn't matter what age you are; these couples are of all ages. You don't have to go to business school; these couples come from all backgrounds. There are many reasons for opening a business and many kinds of businesses to open. It can be a large operation or one run by two. Some of these couples have stayed small, and others have grown big and want to be bigger yet.

What they have in common is that they all work very hard. They all have their struggles. But they are fulfilling a dream. No matter what happens in the rest of their lives, they will know that they realized something others only fantasize about. They have learned what it takes to turn a dream into reality.

2

To Buy or to Build

What Kind of Business
Are You Looking For?

You've decided that you want to open your own business. Whether you know what kind of business you want or just know that you want to open a business, now is the time for research. It is of critical importance to do your footwork. This is where the dream turns to action.

Where do you want to open your business? Do you know what industry you want to be in? What do you want to sell? Do you have a unique idea? Do you have a hobby or an idea that you can transform into a business? Do you want to create the business from scratch, or do you want to buy an existing business? If you want to buy a business, what can you afford? Are you both in agreement?

All the couples highlighted in this book wanted to stay in

Vermont. Some wanted a business because they knew they wouldn't be able to find viable employment to keep them in their desired location. Others opened theirs because they wanted the autonomy of being an owner. Of the ten companies highlighted in this book, two of them bought a business, while the rest created their enterprises. The two that bought, The Herb Patch and Bread & Chocolate, got more *and* less of what they bargained for. Their stories are illustrative of the options and dilemmas you face when buying another business owner's creation.

Bread & Chocolate—The Facts

When Fran and Jonathan Rutstein were ready to go into business, they knew they wanted it to be in Vermont. They had left their hometown of Burlington, Vermont, in 1970 in an orange Volkswagen Bug to see the country. They had lived in California, Iowa, and Colorado and were now ready to settle down in Vermont. Jonathan, fifty-three, had two masters degrees, one in Urban Planning and the other an MBA. Fran, forty-three, had been a teacher. When they returned to Vermont in 1988 they had been married for twelve years and had one son, Aaron.

The business they bought, Bread & Chocolate, started with four chocolate sauces. In the early days Jonathan would make, package, sell, and deliver the product personally, with help from Fran when she wasn't teaching. They first ran their business out of their home, and then in rented space. Fran gave up her teaching job two years after they started the business. She is head of production and employee relations, while Jonathan heads sales and marketing. They employ between four and twenty-four employees, depending on the season. In October 1995 they bought a 9,000-square-foot building in Wells River, Vermont, and for the first time have all operations under one roof.

Today their line includes eight chocolate sauces, Maple Moose

Jonathan and Fran Rutstein

Pop lollipops, chocolate confections, cocoas, lemonade mixes, iced-tea mixes, mustards, and barbecue sauces. They make their chocolate sauces and pops on the premises, while the rest of the products are made by co-packers. They sell directly to consumers and through distributors to retailers. Jonathan reports that in the first year of business they grossed $30,000 and in 1995, $750,000. They service more than 3,000 accounts.

Of 600 accounts, 6 were active

Jonathan Rutstein had been raised in the family's cheese-processing business in Burlington. He was used to hearing business conversation at his dinner table every night. From an early age Jonathan knew he wanted to be in business, but he didn't know what it would be. It was Jonathan's dream to go into business, and Fran was always supportive.

When Fran and Jonathan began their search for a business, they weren't committed to any particular kind. The plan was to return from Colorado to Vermont, where Fran would get a teaching job, and Jonathan would begin the search. Initially he tried an advertising venture, selling ads promoting tourist sites to hotels, motels, and recreational facilities. After two weeks he discovered that not only wasn't he interested in that line of work, but he also didn't think it was a very good idea.

In 1988, Jonathan read an advertisement in a trade journal for a business called Bread & Chocolate. What was being offered was a small specialty food company with no assets, 600 accounts, and four chocolate sauces. The price was right. They plunged in only to discover that only 6 of the 600 listed accounts were still active. What they did actually purchase was the recipes for four chocolate sauces, a name, and a few contacts.

"Basically," admits Fran, "we bought a marketing plan."

Fran and Jonathan built on what they bought, introducing new products annually.

"People who are going into business are looking for a challenge. And then they spend all their time looking for ways out of a challenge."
—JONATHAN RUTSTEIN

Mimi's Magnificent Brownies

Mimi is a neighbor of Jonathan and Fran Rutstein who developed this wonderful brownie recipe using their heavenly cocoa.

1/4 pound (1 stick) butter

1/2 cup sugar

3/4 cup Heavenly Cocoa

2 eggs

1 teaspoon vanilla extract

1/2 cup flour

1 cup chopped nuts

1/4 cup powdered sugar

1. Melt the butter over medium heat in a saucepan. Remove from heat. Stir in the sugar and cocoa until smooth.

2. In a large mixing bowl beat the eggs and vanilla extract. Add the melted chocolate mixture and mix well. Add flour and nuts, stir to combine.

3. Pour into greased and floured 8-x-8-inch pan.

4. Bake at 350 degrees for 20 to 25 minutes, until toothpick in center comes out dry. Let pan cool on rack before cutting. Cut into 4-x-1-inch bars. Dust with powdered sugar.

Makes 16 Brownies

Diane and Richard Copley on Cancun and Ferocious

The Herb Patch Ltd.—The Facts

Diane and Richard Copley bought The Herb Patch, Ltd., in 1986. The company is located in a barn on a fifty-two-acre farm in a mostly agricultural valley in southern Vermont. Included in the purchase was an 1860 farmhouse in which they still live. Richard, fifty, was a full-time cameraman for NBC. For the first two years of the business he commuted from New York City to Vermont on the weekends. In 1988 he left his position to become a freelance cameraman, which he still is today. Diane, forty-nine, has been full-time at The Herb Patch from the beginning. Before that she was a volunteer for many charitable organizations and mother to her son, Rob, from her first marriage. Diane and Richard, both from Memphis, Tennessee, have been married for sixteen years.

When they bought the business, the product line consisted of herbal potpourri and vinegars. The line has evolved to include culinary herbal blends; herbal, fruit and spicy vinegars; flavored honeys; herbal teas; Country Cow Cocoa in nine flavors; Cowpuccino Toppers for hot drinks; Cowpuccino candy bars; cow accessories; and an herbal freshener with cedar chips to protect clothes. They package the vinegars and herbal blends themselves, and the other products are produced by co-packers. Diane reports that in the first *year of business they grossed $160,000 and in 1995, they topped $400,000. Of the five employees who came with the business, three are still employed by them. Today they have five to ten employees, depending on the season.*

Diane is president of the corporation. She is the detail person who heads production and daily operations. Richard is vice president, who, in between freelance camera jobs, works on marketing strategy, sales, and deliveries. They both work on product development.

They bought a business advertised in The New York Times

Diane and Richard Copley wanted out of the fast lane. They were ready for a change of life. The real estate market was up, so when they sold their house in Westchester, they had a modest investment to make in a home and a business. Both love Vermont and describe themselves as risk takers. Diane got into the habit of clipping ads for businesses from newspapers. For a couple of years Richard and Diane explored Vermont looking at country stores and bed-and-breakfasts, one of which they almost bought. They first saw The Herb Patch in February 1986, through a blinding snowstorm. They fell in love at first site.

When it was time to negotiate with the previous owner, they brought the proposal to a lawyer.

"We might not have known anything about the food business, but we knew enough to find a good lawyer," Richard said.

Four months later, in June 1986, Diane and Richard moved to Vermont. They negotiated a five-year noncompeting clause, and Diane was to receive one month's training from the owner. The Herb Patch changed hands smoothly, with business continuing as usual.

By July they were back in New York City hawking their herb blends, vinegars, and potpourris at the New York Fancy Food Show, the largest and most important trade show in the specialty food industry.

It was the late eighties, and the specialty food industry was hot. There were gourmet food shop owners and distributors from all over the country looking for new products. Richard and Diane took turns working the booth and walking the aisles, able to see their competition and the scope of the industry they had just entered. Thus they got a quick introduction into the world of specialty foods.

They returned to their new home in Vermont with a stack of orders and were ready to plunge in. But then . . .

One week after they returned from the food show, the barn that stood one hundred feet behind their home and housed their business ignited in an electrical fire. The Herb Patch burned to the ground.

They lost almost everything: all the product necessary to fill the orders from the show, the original artwork for the labels, packaging and promotional materials, and office equipment. The structure, built in the 1800s was completely destroyed. The business they had bought and were just starting to understand was no more.

By the following morning the fire was extinguished. Exhausted and shocked, the Copleys began to take stock of the loss.

Because of the metal fireproof cabinets, they were able to salvage many of the orders, paperwork, and some checks. For days they dried the sodden documents on a hillside in the sun.

They moved the business into their house. They called their

> "We call our business the Foremost Disaster Company."
> —RICHARD COPLEY

suppliers and co-packers who, after hearing about their plight, put all other projects on hold to fulfill their needs. In a matter of days they had new product, labels, and bottles. In timely fashion, they filled every order they had received at the show.

This catastrophe really put things in perspective quickly. The Copleys learned the lesson of backing up all essential files and keeping them in another location. They also have copies of their artwork off site. Every night, they secure their fireproof file cabinets before they flick the light switch off and cross the lawn to their home from their rebuilt barn.

But this wasn't the only challenge Diane and Richard were to face. In their meeting with the accountant who took care of the books for The Herb Patch they learned that only half of the six hundred customers who supposedly were active buyers really were. Then they discovered that there was money missing from The Herb Patch account.

All fingers pointed at the previous owner. They brought legal action against her and settled out of court. The money, which could have been used to expand the business, was split three ways: one-third for the lawyer, one-third for the accountant, and one-third for Diane and Richard.

The Trials and Tribulations of Buying a Business

You can buy any size business you want, depending on what kind of money you want to spend. Jon and Fran bought a name and four recipes. Richard and Diane purchased property, a home, and a running business—complete with employees.

A business like The Herb Patch offers an up-and-running enterprise, already past the pains of starting a new operation from scratch. It already had a product line, inventory, an office, phones, desks, a customer base, vendors, and established business procedures. Many of the kinks had been ironed out.

But the Copleys inherited someone else's mistakes. They discovered that at any given time a business can be carrying old inventory, out-of-date promotional material, and less-than-effective employees. The seller may misrepresent his or her business, either intentionally or through ignorance.

A fire, misrepresentation of accounts, and the loss of cash were a pretty rude introduction to small-business ownership for the Copleys. And for Jonathan and Fran Rutstein, what they thought would be a thriving little business turned out to be an expensive marketing plan.

Because both couples had saved and planned before they bought their businesses, their early setbacks did not jeopardize their future. Both couples bought businesses that they felt they could afford. They built in safeguards. One of the spouses in each couple kept a full-time job for the first few years of business, affording them a regular income and health insurance.

Both couples adapted and rolled with the punches, surviving early setbacks, and have come to understand some of the basic guidelines that are required when buying a business:

- Seek out a business in a field that you'll enjoy and with which you have at least some familiarity.
- Don't buy the first thing that comes along. No matter what you think, as a buyer you have the leisure to take the time to make the right decision.

- Ask questions—lots of questions—and listen to the answers. Get everything in writing.
- Seek advice (see Appendix) from professionals before you sign on the dotted line.
- Hire a good lawyer who has experience in small business.

Where to Find a Business

Newspapers

Industry trade magazines and newsletters

Industry associations

Professionals in community (bankers, lawyers, etc.)

Vendors and suppliers

Friends

Business owners (they will know of businesses for sale in their industry)

Business brokers

Venture capitalists

Starting from Scratch

If buying into someone else's dream is not what you've had in mind, you're probably thinking of turning your own idea into a moneymaking venture. When you start your own business you'll have the advantage of knowing every step intimately. You'll be doing everything from the ground up—creating a name and a product, finding vendors and customers, and setting up the books and calculating pricing. You'll also run the risk that the idea won't sell.

Do your homework. Read about starting a business. Take a

Award-Winning Chili Verde Parness

"Herb Patch Hombres Take Top Chili," reads the news from the Herb Patch Patter, *a homespun newspaper printed by Richard and Diane once every few years. 1993 was something to write about. That was the year they won the Poultney, Vermont, Annual Chili Cookoff Contest with the following recipe.*

2 tablespoons olive oil

2 medium onions, chopped

4 cloves garlic, diced

4 pork loins, cut into 1/4-inch cubes

1 cup wine, beer or water

1 tablespoon Herb Patch Mexican Ole Blend

4 ounces chopped green chilies (1 can)

2 green peppers, seeded and chopped

3 medium red potatoes, diced

1 pound corn, fresh or frozen

1. Heat olive oil in a deep, heavy skillet. Add the onions and garlic. Cook on low heat until translucent (about 15 minutes). Add the cubed pork and brown on all sides.

2. Add wine, beer or water and Mexican Ole Blend seasoning, chilies, green peppers, potatoes and corn.

3. Cover and simmer for one hour. Add water if necessary. The stew is ready when the pork is tender.

Makes 4 Servings

class at a local college or through an adult education program. Contact the Small Business Administration (SBA) closest to you (see Appendix). The SBA has plenty of material to help you realize your dream, from writing a business plan to conducting a highway density study to find the best location. Research other businesses like the one you want to open. Make sure there is a market for your idea.

Is there room for another product? What is your competition? What are your own passions? Can you marry these to your experience? At what do you excel? What do you like to do? How much money will you need? Where do you want to open your business? With how much risk are you comfortable? What is the growth potential of your idea? If it doesn't work, will you be able to walk away? Do you and your spouse agree on all these things?

One of the attractions of creating a business in Vermont is the support the state gives small businesses (see Appendix). Vermont is a state based on agriculture where small and family-owned businesses are a way of life. Sherrie and Hugh Maurer of Jasmine & Bread used this support when they decided to turn one of Sherrie's hobbies into a business. So did Jon Altman and Carol Berry when they decided to start their business, Putney Pasta.

Jasmine & Bread—The Facts

Sherrie Maurer, fifty-six, grew up in the inner city in Indianapolis, Indiana. She met Hugh, fifty-four, in Yellow Springs, Ohio, where they were working in the same school: she in the office, he as a teacher. They have been married for twenty-five years. In 1970 they moved to an old farmhouse on forty-six acres of land next to a river in Sharon, Vermont. Hugh went into construction, and Sherrie worked in the food industry, as a cook, caterer, and restaurant manager. In 1982 Sherrie won a discrimination suit against a former employer. This incident and the subsequent settlement, along with Hugh's strong encouragement, prompted Sherrie to go into business.

With $5,000 and a combination of loans from family members and a small loan from the local bank, Jasmine & Bread, Inc., was created in 1983. Sherrie and Hugh run the business from their home; they sell directly to their customers by mail and at craft fairs. Most of their ten products are made in their own kitchen. They are: Beyond Catsup, a tomato-apple ketchup; Beyond Belief, a tomato-pear-ginger salsa; Plum Perfect, a sassy sweet-and-sour sauce; Beyond Horseradish Mustard; White Lightning, prepared horseradish; Horseradish Jelly; three barbecue sauces, Caribbean Heat, Bourbon Blast, and Serious Hickory; and Beyond Marinara, a tomato-orange marinara sauce. Their daughter Lauree, thirty-six, works as the production manager.

Hugh and Sherrie Maurer

Sherrie reports that in their first year of business they grossed $5,000 and in their best, $250,000.

In 1989 Sherrie won the New England Small Business Association's Minority Small Business Person of the Year Award.

Sherrie knew she was a fine cook

Sherrie Maurer is a talented woman. As a hobby, she made vegetable and fruit condiments out of the surplus harvest of their vegetable garden. One year, with a bumper crop of apples and tomatoes, Sherrie created what was to be her first gourmet product, Beyond Catsup, a tomato and apple ketchup sweetened with maple syrup. She gave away bottles of Beyond Catsup as gifts. Everyone raved about the taste and asked for more.

When the Maurers decided to open a business, using Sherrie's talent made sense. Neither Sherrie nor Hugh had experience or background in business, so they sought help from the Department of Agriculture and local businesspeople. Sherrie tackled her fledgling business like a good student, pen and pad in hand at all times.

"There is always someone who says to you, 'If there is anything that I can do for you, let me know.' So many people let that pass. I go back to them and ask, 'What *can* you do for me?' " Sherrie explained. "I have so many mentors."

She bartered with her lawyer. She got advice, and he received Tomato-Apple Catsup or Beyond Horseradish Mustard. She visited with her banker every few weeks, just to listen to him talk about business.

"He was happy to share his knowledge with me if I was bold enough to ask for it," Sherrie said.

"*Bold*—that's a good word," Hugh adds. "Be bold."

Carol Berry and Jonathan Altman

Putney Pasta—The Facts

Jonathan Altman, forty-seven, originally from New York City, and Carol Berry, forty-six, who grew up in Rhode Island, met in college, married, and moved to Vermont in the late seventies. After their son, Justin, was born in 1981, they decided to open a business in order to stay in Vermont. Jon's grandfather was the original manufacturer of Nathan's Coney Island Hot Dogs. Carol's family was in the restaurant and hotel business. In 1983, with a $30,000 loan, they opened Putney Pasta, a vegetarian pasta company, in a converted barn on their property in Putney, Vermont.

They incorporated in 1983, with Jon as president and Carol as vice president. Today Jon is CEO and Carol is president. They began production with eight different pastas and three sauces. Today they have over forty pastas and seven sauces, ranging from tortellini filled with spinach and walnuts to ravioli stuffed with Gorgonzola cheese. Their sauces range from Alfredo Sauce to Sweet Red Pepper Sauce. They manufacture all the products themselves.

Jonathan heads sales and marketing. Initially he sold directly and made all the deliveries. Now he uses common carriers and sells exclusively through distributors. Carol is in charge of manufacturing, finances, and day-to-day operations.

During the first year of business they had one employee and

grossed $150,000. By 1993 they were employing eighteen people full-time and reporting gross earnings over $2,500,000. In 1993, Carol and Jon moved to a 41,000-square-foot plant with a separate office building on twenty-one acres of land in Chester, Vermont. Today, with forty full-time employees, their sales are over $5,000,000 annually.

**"We went after what we thought was
a small niche in the market,
and it turned out to be larger than we thought."**
—JONATHAN ALTMAN

Understanding the food business

Carol and Jon both come from families of people who worked for themselves. They both had been employed in the food industry. But when they decided to open a business, food was not their first or favorite idea. Except for a sudden flash of common sense, Carol and Jon might be marketing decorative sponges today. They followed their heads and decided to build on their experience and interests. Jon had already been exposed to his grandfather's business and was taking classes at the New York Restaurant School where one of his professors encouraged him to consider the frozen food industry.

In the early 1980s, the popularity of pasta was really beginning to boom. It had come a long way from spaghetti and meatballs. It was a versatile, inexpensive, and universally loved food with lots of potential in a fast-growing gourmet marketplace. And since Jon is a vegetarian, the idea of creating an all-natural, vegetarian pasta line fit the couple's interests, experience, and passions perfectly.

Putney Pasta would also reach a burgeoning market of sophisticated consumers who wanted "fast" food that was good, healthy, and as close to homemade as one could get in packaged food.

Pick a Product You Like (and Know Something About)

Both Sherrie and Hugh and Jonathan and Carol built their businesses from something that fell within their experience and talents. Sherrie was a great cook who knew people enjoyed her product. Although she had no experience in business, she wasn't afraid to ask for help. Jon had experience in the food-manufacturing business and received further information through formal training.

All four are members of the Specialty Food Association of Vermont, where they get help and support on an ongoing basis. Neither of these couples started out over their heads. They took calculated risks, and started with a size of business with which they were comfortable—Jasmine & Bread in their home, and Putney Pasta in a barn on their property.

Whether you buy a business or create one from scratch, make sure it is something that you like. People who do what they like are happier. You will be spending more time at it than you think. Each couple reports that they underestimated the amount of time that running their own business would take.

This is your creation. Make it work for you.

The Pros and Cons of Buying or Building a Business

TO BUY	TO BUILD
Pros	*Pros*
Skip slow growth of a new business	Start off with a clean slate
Acquire product and customer base	Grow gradually as you're ready to
Have established vendors and suppliers	Create the organization you want
Systems in place	Hire own staff
Cons	*Cons*
Inherit someone else's mistakes	Have to do everything from scratch
Not always clear what you are buying	Takes longer to get up to speed
May cost more money to buy	Longer time to build customer base
Buying someone else's dream	Credit and other resources may not be readily available

3

Getting the Business Started

This is it: the door that must be opened in order to realize a viable company. It is time to structure the legal organization, decide on ownership, and raise money. These kinds of cut-and-dried business decisions are where any concept needs to become a reality. A couple will have to separate their personal relationship from these kinds of business decisions.

You have the product, and you know the location. It's time to pull together all the pieces that you will need to structure your business. What type of legal structure will be best? Who will own the business—both of you or just one of you? What is a business plan? What purpose does it serve? How do you write one? How much money do you really need to open and run the business? Where can money be found?

What Business Structure Will Work Best for You?

It is important to gather information before deciding on what kind of legal structure would be best for the business. This is the time to talk to an accountant and a business lawyer. Don't make this decision without being educated.

There are three basic types of legal organization: proprietorship, partnership, and corporation. A proprietorship has a single owner. Legally, the business and person are one. For a couple in business, this limits the ownership to only one of the spouses. With a partnership there may be more than one owner. As in a proprietorship, all partners are liable for the activities of the business. The profits and losses, assets and liabilities are the partners'.

The third type is a corporation. It is a taxable entity unto itself and offers the most protection in terms of liability. Think of it as a person responsible for its own taxes and liable for its own actions. There is a special corporation called a sub–chapter S corporation in which the owners report the income in their personal tax returns. An S corporation has limitations. It must be a domestic corporation, is limited to thirty-five shareholders, and the shareholders must be individuals. A company can start as an S corporation and then opt to become a regular corporation at a later date. This is a good option for a small business because the owners can benefit from any losses of a start-up operation until the business is making a profit.

There is a fourth option that is newly available in some states. It is called a limited liability company (LLC). This offers insulation from personal liability, is taxed as a partnership and has certain rights usually available only to a corporation.

Many businesses start out as proprietorships, partnerships, or sub-chapter S corporations and become regular corporations as they grow, become profitable, and increase in liability. If there are substantial personal assets to protect or a large amount of exposure due to the nature of the business, it may be wise to incorporate immediately. There is no right or wrong answer, just the one that fits you and your business best.

What is the nature of your business and your liability? How big is your exposure? Do you have personal assets that you want to protect? As a couple, do both of you need or want ownership? Is there a reason it would be best to have all ownership in one name?

There are many good books that will explain in detail the nature of the different legal forms. The better informed you are, the better decision you will make. Choose knowledgeably. Once you get into the day-to-day running of the business, the structure you will have created becomes the backbone of your endeavor (see Resources in the Appendix).

At *Highland Sugarworks,* Jim and Judy MacIsaac had to work out the issue of ownership and legal status a few years after the business had been started.

Judy and Jim MacIsaac with son, Dylan

Highland Sugarworks—The Facts

Highland Sugarworks is a corporation owned by Jim (thirty-eight) and Judy (thirty-one) MacIsaac. They sell 100 percent pure maple syrup; pure maple specialties including maple sugar, maple butter, and maple candy; and Vermont honey and pancake mix.

Originally from Weston, Connecticut, Jim had been skiing in Vermont his whole life. He knew this was where he wanted to live. After graduating from the University of Vermont with a degree in dairy technology, Jim worked in the dairy industry, as a plant manager, and tried a stint of selling agricultural insurance to farmers. What he really wanted was his own business.

Jim started the business in 1986 on his family's hobby farm by tapping maple trees and selling bulk syrup. In 1987 he started to package his syrup for retail sale, which netted him a higher return. After three years of doubling his volume, Jim began to supplement his harvest by buying syrup from area farmers and packaging it for retail sales. Today the syrup that Jim makes comprises only 10 percent of all the syrup Highland sells. With a start-up loan of $10,000 from Jim's parents, Highland Sugarworks has grown into the third-largest distributor of maple syrup in Vermont.

Judy, originally from New Jersey, met Jim in 1989. When they were married in 1991, she began to work full-time at Highland

Sugarworks. Her background in retail sales and marketing brought complementary skills to Jim's technological and financial strengths.

In 1996 Jim and Judy moved the business from the sugar shack on Jim's family's farm to a 10,000-square-foot building which they lease in Websterville, Vermont, thirty miles from their home in Waitsfield.

Jim started the business, but Judy needed equal ownership

When Judy started working for Highland Sugarworks, she threw herself into her work. Jim was thrilled. Here was a smart person whose wages he could afford—none. She brought to the business an extensive background in retail sales. When she wasn't helping Jim pack maple syrup, she was working on a marketing plan that included more sophisticated packaging, new products, and an expanded customer base.

It was easy to divide the responsibilities between the two of them. Their domains were clear: Judy was in charge of all sales and marketing, and Jim headed up production and financing. They each had the final say in their own arenas. They trusted each other's decisions and abilities. Their rule of thumb in a quandary was: "Your first guess is your best guess."

But Judy had no ownership. Jim had started the business and run it for five years before he met Judy. He had set up a proprietorship that worked well for him. It was his business, and he didn't want to give up any ownership. He couldn't understand why she needed the legal ownership. "It's the same thing as if you did own it," he would say. "We're married and it's our business."

Judy needed ownership. It was very important to her that her name be on the papers. She needed a stake in the action. Jim gradually came to understand how important this was to Judy. For the future of their business and marriage, he acquiesced. Today, with the incorporation of their business, they are equal shareholders.

Every couple and company is different. Not all have equal ownership, and with some, only one partner owns all. When deciding upon ownership and legal organization get advice. Oftentimes the facts of the situation will determine the type of organization that is best for the couple and company.

What Is a Business Plan?

A business plan is a document that explains what your business will be and how it will become profitable. For the person new to business, it is an excellent learning tool. It is also a sales tool to help sell your idea to potential investors and a requirement for borrowing money from any financial institution.

This map of your new business will show you how every aspect of your business relates to every other aspect. It will reveal areas where capital is needed that you might not have considered previously. It can show you in which direction you need to head. It's what they teach in business school, over and over again.

The plan is fact filled: who will own the business, what you will be selling, where it will be. It is also full of projections: how much you will need to open your business; how much you think you can sell; how much you have to sell to cover your costs; what it will cost to produce your product; what your overhead expenses will be; and how long it will take to turn a profit. You will do a pro forma income statement, where you will be estimating costs

Legal Forms of Organization

Sole Proprietorship—One owner

ADVANTAGES

Simplest form of legal structure

Little or no government approval

Owner is taxed as an individual at a lower rate than a corporation

DISADVANTAGES

Owner is personally liable for all business activity

Owner pays self-employment tax

General Partnership—Two or more partners

ADVANTAGES

Easy to form

An entity separate from owners

Owners are taxed as individuals at a lower rate than a corporation

Two or more partners bring different strengths and abilities to business

DISADVANTAGES

Partners are personally liable for all business activity

Limited Partnership—A general partner and limited partner(s)

General partner may be liable for all business activity, limited partner(s) liable only to the extent of his/her contributions

Limited Liability Company (LLC)

ADVANTAGES

Insulation from liability

Taxed as partnership but has rights of corporation

DISADVANTAGES

Available in only forty states

Sub–Chapter S Corporation

Created for small businesses—taxed like partnership

Has limitations on it when raising capital that regular corporations do not have

(continued)

> *Corporation—A legal entity separate from all partners/shareholders*
>
> ADVANTAGES
>
> Corporation becomes person under law and pays its own taxes
>
> Owners have limited liability
>
> Easier to raise capital
>
> DISADVANTAGES
>
> More expensive to start and maintain
>
> Corporations are regulated by government
>
> Corporation taxes are higher than individual taxes

and sales. You will do a cash-flow chart, and from it you will learn the cause and effect of incoming cash and outgoing expenses. These numbers will tell you how much you need to start your business and see it through until it can support itself.

There is a fine line between optimistic and unrealistic projections. Of course you believe you will be a success, and you hope to be an instant success. And you might be. But more often, it takes time. Accumulating sales and customers is a process. Be reasonable, and err on the conservative side. It's best not to set yourself up with unrealistic expectations. Better to come in over planned projections.

There are many excellent books on business plans, as well as computer software. The Small Business Administration has material and can offer help. Another great organization is the Service Corps of Retired Executives (SCORE—see Appendix). These retired businesspeople have experience from which you can benefit greatly.

You can approach the plan as a necessary evil in order to get someone to give you money, or you can look at it as an invaluable learning tool and an important step in building a business. The more you put into the plan, the more you'll get out of it. Consider it a road map, and a necessity when applying for commercial loans. Writing a business plan will force you to sit down and consider all the aspects of a business. It will also teach you something about what you are getting yourself into!

Owner Jacki Baker and husband Ron Mancini from *Mother Myrick's* helped the bank understand their vision by writing a very detailed business plan when they were expanding their confectionery and ice cream shop.

Mother Myrick's—The Facts

I n 1977 Ron Mancini moved to Vermont and began to make fudge for his friend Sandra Ryan on a marble table behind a large window overlooking a sidewalk in the tourist town of Manchester. Candy making was a far cry from the insurance business he had left behind in New York City. Within a year, Mother Myrick's moved to its present location and opened as an ice cream and confectionery parlor. The ice cream company, Purity Ice Cream, loaned Sandra $21,000 and when the business needed more money, Vermont Bank gave the company an additional $12,000.

In 1978 Jacki Baker moved to Vermont from Newport, Rhode Island. She was introduced to Ron by her roommate, Susanella, a sometime employee of Mother Myrick's. One day Jacki walked in when the shop was packed and pitched in to help. She was hooked. Jacki and Ron began to date and married in 1980. That same year Sandra sold Jacki 30 percent of Mother Myrick's for $3,800.

In 1983 Sandra sold the rest of the business to Jacki for $30,000 with a ten-year note, making Jacki full owner of Mother Myrick's. That year Jacki applied for and received a loan of $172,000 from the Bank of Vermont to expand the store by 1,100 square feet, bringing the total space to 1,700 square feet.

During the first year of expansion Mother Myrick's grossed $125,000. By the late eighties retail and mail-order sales had

Ron Mancini and Jacki Baker

grown to $400,000. In 1995 the store grossed over $900,000. To-
day they have sixteen employees.

They sell homemade candy and confections, Purity Ice Cream,
cakes, and pastries. Jacki, forty-eight, heads up the confectionery,
candy kitchen, and mail-order operation. Ron, fifty-three, is in
charge of the Parlor Cafe, bakery, finances, and advertising. They
work together on marketing.

A business plan helped the bank
understand their vision

Mother Myrick's success comes from a combination of good timing, hard work, high expectations from the key players, and an
optimal location. But to create that combination they needed to
be funded and needed to convince the bank that Mother Myrick's
was going to be successful.

In 1983, with Ron's input, Jacki created a business plan. They
needed to help the bank understand how a five-foot-long candy
case had created sales of $50,000 in one year, and how they knew
they could grow this number successfully.

Their business plan included a sales history of the first five
years of Mother Myrick's, profit and loss statements, a five-year
projection, an estimate of leasehold improvements, and equipment purchases. And a narrative of their vision.

In the narrative they highlighted market trends. Eating ice
cream was becoming a national pastime. In the late 1970s companies like Steve's in Boston and Häagen-Dazs in New York had
developed a market for gourmet ice cream. In the early '80s Go-
diva chocolate hit the market, educating Americans about high-
quality chocolates. Also in the '80s, American cuisine was coming

into its own, and with that, American pastry. Ron and Jacki could feel the tide rising and were ready to respond.

"Writing the proposal clarified for me what I had in my mind's eye," Jacki said. "It gave us the tools we needed to go forward once the loan was secured. The bank wants you to do a plan for your own benefit. It organizes thought and creates a format to make action possible. One important aspect of doing the projections was scheduling the loan payments that were reasonable for us."

Besides their good timing and good location, they loved what they were doing, they loved being together, and were committed to top quality and excellent service.

Ron learned early in his life about high-quality retail shops. His father, Joe, had been a salesman for Brooks Brothers in New York City for sixty-six years. Ron had worked there when he was a teenager.

Jacki had grown up in a home where her parents had worked together in a pool business for thirteen years. When they retired they bought a motel. Customer service is in her blood, as well.

"Our underlying theme is always to do whatever it takes. You just do it," Ron said.

No Matter Where the Financing Comes From, There Are Strings Attached

It takes money to start a business. Probably much more than you think. One of the major causes of business failure is lack of capital. The time to plan for this is before you open. You'll need enough start-up capital to open your doors and to keep you going until sales translate into cash. And then you'll find yourself on the cash-

The Nuts and Bolts of a Business Plan

Description of the Business

   What you are selling

   Who will buy from you

   Where you will be located

   When you will open

   Why you will be a success

Marketing and Sales Plan

   Explanation of marketing strategy

   Pricing

   Sales tactics

   Advertising and promotion

Personnel

   Explanation of key management team

   Proposed labor force

Who You Are

   Your professional resume

   Your personal background—including your strengths and weaknesses

   Your personal financial statement

Financial Projections

   Start-up Expenses

   Pro forma balance sheet

   Profit and loss forecast

   Cash-flow projections

flow treadmill—the least favorite and one of the most important exercises of every business. Cash flow is the pulse of your business.

How much money do you need to open your business? How much will you need to maintain it until it can generate enough to pay the bills? Where are you going to get it? How much can you afford to borrow? How can you keep costs low? What are the hidden expenses that, if you've never run a business, you wouldn't know about? What are the necessities? How much do you need for your personal life? How much money do you want to make?

There are many sources of money, from savings to bank loans, and some sources you might not have considered. You may borrow money personally, or through your business, using equipment, real estate, cash receivables, or other assets as collateral. As a new business, without a track record, you will be asked for a personal guarantee.

Lending money is the business of financial institutions. They lend money in order to make money. They are experts. They understand what it takes to make a business work. They also know the failure rate and know how to protect themselves. This is not without risk. The number of bankruptcies in this country has grown. They know this, too. Some of the interest you will pay on loans is to cover this loss. They understand that there is a chance that they will lose money. They try to minimize this chance, but it still exists. If the worst-case scenario unfolds, and they lose, they write it off. The risk is high and they try to mitigate that risk by selecting "safe bet" customers and charging interest sufficient to cover their failures and still make a profit. It's your job to make them confident that your business will not become one of their write-offs.

Then there are the angels—your friends and relatives who want to help you, want you to succeed. Although it may seem easier to borrow from those you know, and without as much documentation, the strings attached may be more binding. When borrowing from family and friends, there is added risk: not only might they lose money in your venture, but your relationship may also be affected. What if you borrow $25,000 from your mother and things don't work out and you can't pay her back? Can she fiscally tolerate the loss? How about your relationship? What is your tolerance for guilt? When borrowing from those you love, be prepared for the worst. Talk about the downside. Hope it will never happen. But if it does, you'll be better off for having prepared for it ahead of time.

Dave Lyon, Lynne Andreen and son, J. B. Lyon from *Uncle Dave's Kitchen* have learned a lot about borrowing money, both from banks as well as friends and relatives.

Lynne Andreen and David Lyon

Uncle Dave's Kitchen—The Facts

U ncle Dave's Kitchen was founded in 1988 by Lynne Andreen and stepson J.B. Lyon. A year later, the company's namesake, Dave, joined son, J.B., and wife, Lynne. In 1994 J.B. left to get his MBA, leaving Dave and Lynne to run the company. Dave heads sales and Lynne heads production and oversees the employees. They work on marketing and hiring together.

Production of the all-natural products started in the kitchen of Lynne and Dave's home. Within a year they moved to an office, decided to be a marketing company, and hired a co-packer to produce their line, a range of sauces, condiments, and snack foods including their Original Ketchup and Kickin' Ketchup, Kickin' Mustard, Kickin' Grill Sauce, Zippy Fixin's, Excellent Marinara Sauce (their biggest seller), Uncle Dave's Jumbo Peanuts, and Carrot-Horseradish. They sell directly to consumers and, through distributors, to retailers all over the country. In 1994 they bought their own building in South Londonderry, Vermont, five miles from their home on Stratton Mountain.

Dave, sixty-two, is an entrepreneur who has started and run many businesses, and Lynne, forty-eight, has an extensive background in sales and marketing. Uncle Dave's initial financing was a $10,000 commercial bank loan, $2,000 from Dave (before he officially joined the business), and $500 from a cousin. In 1992 *they sold 15 percent of their corporation to friends and family to raise $250,000. They work with a line of credit from a local bank and a guaranteed SBA loan. Dave reports that in 1989 the company grossed $100,000 and in 1995 they grossed almost $2,000,000. In 1993 they made a profit for the first time. They have five employees.*

They raised money from friends and family

Dave, Lynne, and J.B. made the decision to stop producing their own products and get out of the manufacturing side of the business for two reasons: One, they didn't have the capital to buy the proper equipment to produce the volume and variety of product they had developed and would develop; and two, they didn't want to be in the manufacturing business, period. Their strength lay in marketing, and they knew it.

"I didn't want the headaches of manufacturing. I've done it before, and knew I didn't want to," said Dave.

Uncle Dave's is an example of a company undercapitalized from the start. The $12,500 start-up money was not nearly enough to underwrite their vision. It takes awhile to amass enough customers to generate sufficient cash flow to pay the bills. In the meantime, a lot of money is needed to create, produce, and promote the product. Even when they decided to leave the manufacturing to someone else, they still had to buy and pay for the ingredients and pay the co-packer *before* they had product to sell.

"In the early days we had to pay our suppliers and co-packers before they would even produce the product," Lynne explains. "Our customers won't pay us until thirty days after delivery, so we were constantly crunched for cash."

To raise capital they elected to sell 15 percent of the company. J.B. spent many months creating a business proposal that represented their company, its principles, and a forecast for the future. They valued the company at $1,500,000 and decided to sell 1,000-share units at $15.00 per share. They sold 15 units—raising $225,000—to eleven investors, all friends and family members.

Because Uncle Dave's is a sub–chapter S corporation, all the investors are individuals.

"There is a difference between selling stock to family and friends and borrowing money from them. We have done both," said Lynne Andreen. "When the eleven investors bought stock in Uncle Dave's, they knew the risk involved. We were very clear that there was risk. They all could afford to loan us the money without jeopardizing their lifestyle. But that's not the same as borrowing money from family members. My advice about borrowing from family is *don't*. We did. If I had it to do over again, we wouldn't.

"You know what they say: You can pick your friends but not your family. With family members, if you have borrowed money from them, it becomes part of your relationship. Every time you see them you'll think of it. And it's not always a money issue. It's a relationship issue. I can tell you in one word, it's *guilt*."

Think carefully about where the money will come from . . . whether or not you want to be indebted to family. Owners of some of these businesses have borrowed money from parents and have ended up in litigation. This may not happen to you, but be aware of the potential ramifications of borrowing from family.

It's Never Quite Enough

"Whatever you think you need, double it," said Dave. "And however long you think you will need to break even, double that

Where to Find Money

Personal

Savings

Credit cards

Borrow against insurance policy

Borrow through your stock-
broker

Home equity loan

Friends and family

Business associates

Professional

Banks

Small Business Association (SBA)

Leasing companies

Small business investment
companies

Commercial finance companies

Venture capitalists

State funding programs

Seller of existing business

While Running Your Business

Landlord (may give you free rent for a certain length of time while
you establish yourself)

Customers (may pay when placing order)

Suppliers (may sell to you on credit)

too. That is probably the single most important thing I could tell
anyone about going into business. It's important to ask for all
that you will need now, when you are just starting out. It will be
harder to get money later if you find you have undercapitalized
yourself. You need to look at what your financial situation will
be five years from now, not just at the money you need for today."

One of the reasons that Uncle Dave's raised money from
family and friends was that it was more accessible to them than
corporate investors. Curiously, couples trying to raise money for
a business may find themselves facing a prejudice against couples
in business. Potential investors worry about the couple's relationship adversely affecting the future. What happens if the couple
breaks up? What will happen to the business?

"In the six years I was in business with my parents, I learned that professional investors do not like to invest in couples," said J. B. "It's a no-no. One way to get around this is if you have other top management in your company who have an extremely strong track record in the industry. This creates a balance in the eyes of an investor when there are nonfamily managers. Then the investment community may become interested."

Do your homework. The two major reasons for business failure are undercapitalization and lack of required skills. Make sure you are being realistic, that you are getting as much money as you need. If you are borrowing from financial institutions, be confident that you can live with the terms of the note, that your debt will be manageable. If you are borrowing from friends and family, be clear. Put it in writing. Make sure your agreement with them is legally sound. Don't try to sell a rosy picture just to get what you want. You have to live with the deal you make, long after the money has changed hands.

As a start-up business you'll want to keep costs low. Lease space instead of buying a location. Look for used equipment. Start in a small space. Share services with other companies. If you have less debt, you'll have less pressure. Growth will be easier if it is gradual and exacting, rather than quick and reactive. This will keep the stress more manageable—maybe.

Determine the legal structure of your business, have a thorough business plan, and make a realistic estimate of how much money you need and where you are going to get it. The clearer the picture you have of where you're headed, the less likely you'll be to fall into traps in the future.

4

Who's Running
the Business?

What Are Your Strengths?

A couple brings to their business their individual capabilities, knowledge, skills, and experience. They have the advantage of drawing from two sets of traits. The challenge for the couple is to define their collective strengths and use them advantageously. What are your strengths? What tasks do you enjoy doing? Does one of you love to create order? Who likes to work with numbers? That person may want to be responsible for the bookkeeping. Does one of you enjoy talking with people more than the other? Is that person more tolerant of people's personalities? Is one of you a natural-born salesman? What are your weaknesses? What are the tasks you dislike? Are there areas of business that you just don't understand? Identify these. One of you may have a strength that compensates for the other's weakness. Are there jobs that neither of you likes to do? This is where you may need to hire an employee with those particular skills.

How a couple runs their business depends on the nature of the couple. Look at how you run your household. Is there a definite division of labor? Does one of you always pay the bills? Is one responsible for social engagements? Is it one spouse who always talks to the children's teachers? Or, do you go to the conferences, pay the bills, and decide on activities together after discussing all aspects of a situation? The way you run your marriage will be the way you are inclined to run your business.

While it is a good idea (and often the case) that both spouses are able to perform any task at work, a defined division of labor will help the company run more smoothly.

Whoever is responsible for a given area of the business should also be the person most qualified to make decisions that affect that department. Whoever makes the decision is the person responsible for the outcome. How will you feel if your spouse makes a decision that doesn't turn out well? Will you be able to accept and not condemn him or her for making a bad decision?

Couples either make decisions autonomously or they make them together. With most of these businesses, the day-to-day decisions are made by the spouse most intimately involved with that area of the business, and the large decisions are made together.

Davis and Ellen Koier from Ward's Pond Farm are a couple who like to make the decisions together, although neither of them relishes the responsibility of making decisions. That means that each has to be fully apprised of the ramifications of any decision in order to make the best choice. In a small company like theirs it is easier to make all the decisions together. When a business gets larger, dual decision-making can get more complicated: there is just too much to do for both partners to be intimately involved in every aspect of operations. And, the larger a business the more complexities there are, often involving other people in the decision making besides the spouses.

A couple in business has the benefit of sharing the joys of ownership as well as its burdens—whether the burden be a concern about the bottom line, or how to weather the impact of having to fire an employee, or the need to make a decision that will cost the company money and provide returns that will not be clear until the future. There is someone to bounce ideas off, someone who has just as much of an investment in the outcome as the one making the decision.

Who is going to make the decisions? As a couple how have you made decisions in the past? How do you make decisions? Are they difficult for you to make? Once you make a decision, do you then rehash it?

Some couples in business have other family members who work with them. The dynamic of the husband-and-wife team at work now becomes part of a larger family dynamic at play. In the case of Uncle Dave's, the company was started by Dave's son and Lynne before Dave came on board. How do you keep the boundaries between family members that are necessary to create and maintain a healthy work environment? How do you separate family roles from business roles?

Who's the boss in a business owned by a couple? The answer will vary, depending on the division of duties, the structure of the organization, and the personalities involved. The key question then becomes, How will you divide the responsibility while sharing the burden?

When they created Yesterday's Kitchen, Marilyn Wedig and Harry Haff discovered that their experience and personalities helped define the structure of their business. Marilyn clearly belonged in marketing and sales, and Harry headed production and purchasing.

Harry Haff and Marilyn Wedig

Yesterday's Kitchen—The Facts

*M*arilyn Wedig, fifty-three, and Harry Haff, forty-nine,
opened Yesterday's Kitchen in 1992, one year after they
married. Harry had previously owned and run a bakery in Woodstock, Vermont. Marilyn, originally from California, had spent
many years as an IBM executive before moving to Vermont with
her three daughters.

Yesterday's Kitchen started as a hobby after Harry sold his bakery. Marilyn and Harry would make herbal vinegars and oils and
sell them at the farmers' market. The decision to go into business
came when Harry was offered a job as pastry chef for the Ritz
Carlton in Philadelphia, but Marilyn and Harry decided they
wanted to stay in Vermont and turn their hobby into a business.

Using money from savings and reinvesting the income from
sales, Yesterday's Kitchen grew on a shoestring. In 1993 they rented
warehouse space near their home. Within six months they had outgrown that space and moved the whole production to a 3,400-
square-foot building in West Woodstock, Vermont, where they
stayed for three years. In 1996 they moved the sales and adminis-
trative offices back into their home and shifted production to a
cannery in Waterbury, Vermont. In 1992 their sales were
$15,000. Marilyn reports sales for 1996 of over $300,000.

Yesterday's Kitchen has twenty-nine products including herbal *oils, marmalades, relishes, fruit sauces, and vinegars. They sell di-rectly to customers and through distributors to retailers. They make all their own products. Harry oversees production and purchasing, and Marilyn handles sales and marketing.*

Marilyn and Harry bring complementary skills to the union

Harry has always been creative. After graduating from the Julliard School of Music, he played the trombone professionally for ten years. When he decided to change careers, he attended the Cu-linary Institute of America. After graduating in 1979, he went to Zurich to work as a pastry chef, then worked in New York City as an executive chef before moving to Woodstock, Vermont.

Originally from California, Marilyn moved to Woodstock to escape corporate America. After years as an account executive for IBM, the longtime single mother of three girls wanted to raise her children in Vermont, where she found work selling real estate.

Marilyn and Harry have their areas of expertise. Harry is the chef and production manager. The product is his utmost concern. Marilyn runs the office and is the marketing expert. She is trained to be customer driven. The division of labor is clear.

The real challenge for Marilyn and Harry is making their particular work styles mesh. When Harry tackles a project it's often to the exclusion of the outside world. If he is making Pos-itively Peach Fruit Sauce, his whole mind is wrapped up in this single undertaking. Marilyn works best when three ideas are per-colating in her mind at once. At any given time, she is selling, buying and, with both transactions on hold, needs to know from Harry how many cases of Summer Glory Vinegar are in inven-tory. Harry has no idea, and no inclination to stop what he is doing to find out. Marilyn needs to know *now*. Harry will tell her later.

Unlike some of the other couples who married in their twenties, had children, and started their business together, Marilyn and Harry led separate lives before they opened their business. Adjusting to running a business with a spouse has not been easy for them.

Harry, having owned and operated his own business for five years, knew what kind of work it would take to be successful. But he never had a partner or a wife. Now he had both in one person.

Besides having a partner, Marilyn also had to adjust to the stress inherent in owning a business. There is no buffer zone as there is in a big corporation.

Dave Lyon and Lynne Andreen from Uncle Dave's had warned them. Getting together in midlife and starting a new marriage and a new business is no mean feat. Adapting to each other and accommodating the demands of a fledgling enterprise can create a great amount of stress and tension.

"This is definitely the hardest thing I've ever done," said Marilyn.

Decision Making between Partners

Running a home and family requires that a couple make decisions all the time. Who is going to do the dishes, the shopping, the laundry? How much television will the children be allowed to watch? What is the teenager's curfew? Where will the family go on vacation? There is a working dynamic that the couple will bring with them into their business. It may need some alteration.

In business together, the couple is relying on each other to do the best job they can in order to make enough money to support the business, employees, and the family. Decisions may

Major Areas in a Business: Who's Going to Do What?

RESPONSIBILITY	ROLE	TRAITS
Sales	Sells to customer Customer relations	People person Diplomatic
Marketing and Advertising	Plans how to promote business Creates and protects image	Creative Sensitive
Administrative	Does the paperwork for business Receivables, payables, etc.	Attentive to detail Timely
Financial	Analyzes financial situation Prepares statements, reports Budgets	Analytical Organized
Professional	Communicates with bankers, lawyers, insurance agencies	Confidence Ability to "schmooze"
Employee Relations	Hires and trains employees Mediates difficulties	Patience and empathy People person Leadership qualities
Production	Creates and manages production	Organized

(continued)

Product Development	Develops new products	Creative Resourceful
Purchasing	Buys equipment and material Vendor negotiation	Price conscious Negotiating abilities
Shipping and Receiving	Sets shipping schedules Deliveries Receives shipments	Organized Efficient

become more charged if one or the other partner is afraid that the wrong decision may affect the bottom line, and thus their security. Intertwined in decision making is the ability of each spouse to trust the other. Trust is earned. Decision by decision.

"If I ask my spouse to make a decision, do I have the right to slam her if I don't like it?" Davis Koier, from Ward's Pond Farm asked. "If one of us is willing to make the decision, we can't condemn the other for the decision."

Who makes the decisions and how they are made is different with each couple. Davis and Ellen Koier are an example of a couple who try to share all decisions.

"We trade our decision making back and forth," Davis added. "Sometimes with us, it is whoever is *willing* to make the decision. Sometimes neither of us wants to make it. There are so many. Should we do a show or not? Should we change our pricing? Give a volume discount? Should we cut our mailing list? What new product should we bring in? Should we hire a new person or not? Should we buy that new piece of equipment? Hey, I made the last decision, you make this one!"

They trust each other's ability
to make decisions

"Probably one of the beauties of being a partner with your spouse is no one knows you better than your spouse," said Jonathan Altman from Putney Pasta. Jonathan and Carol have been running their company together for over ten years and have been married for over fifteen. They have clearly defined areas of responsibility. Jonathan has been in charge of sales and marketing from the beginning. He set up all the early accounts and made all the deliveries.

"Who else could I trust to be out there representing our company more than my husband?" Carol said.

Carol was in charge of manufacturing and has become the finance person. It was a skill she discovered that she had as the company grew from a two-person operation to what it is today—a business with over forty employees.

"Carol's judgment really is impeccable," Jonathan said of his wife.

Carol and Jonathan have always trusted each other to make the best decisions for the company. They have proven to each other that they are capable. They have each other's support and ready ear.

Marilyn, from Yesterday's Kitchen, has had to learn how to trust Harry. Marilyn had been on her own for a long time. Her first marriage ended when her three daughters were very young. She had been a successful single parent for many years. Working with a partner was new for her.

"I had to stop going into the production room to check to

make sure that there were no smudges on the bottles," Marilyn said. "I loved Harry and trusted him, so I had to act that way too."

When Extended Family Is Involved

What happens when a member of the family wants to work in the business? Half of the ten couples in the book have had a child work for them at one time or another. Not only has Uncle Dave's employed Dave and Lynne's children, but one of the children, J.B., is an original partner.

Family business is a cornerstone of small business in America. Working with any family member, be it a parent, spouse, sibling, or other relative, immediately brings to the forefront the importance of boundaries between the familial role and the business position. Everyone knows someone whose family has been divided by a business.

Uncle Dave's has been a family affair from the beginning. Besides the fact that the company was started by a son and step-mother who then hired the father/husband, every other child has worked for the company in one capacity or another. Dave's daughter Cynthia, a business consultant, has helped to write business plans. His other daughter, Amy, had a gourmet food shop and sold Uncle Dave's products from day one. Lynne's daughter, Andrea, opened up many important accounts in the early days of Uncle Dave's, and her son, Aaron, has lent them a hand on numerous occasions. Their twelve-year-old grandchild, Max, has worked at craft shows. Even their ex-son-in-law, David, has sold for them.

Family is very important to Dave and Lynne. They have always welcomed their children working at Uncle Dave's, if that is what they wanted to do. One of the motivations for Lynne's having gone into business with J.B. was to help him.

"I saw this as an opportunity for us to bond. He asked me to help, and I said 'yes,' " said Lynne.

Because Dave had worked with his parents in their truck-leasing and warehousing business, it didn't seem strange at all to him to be in business with his son or with his wife. "My father was one of seven brothers. They helped one another out in business. I was in business with my father and mother. When Lynne and J.B. asked me to come to work with them, I jumped in."

From 1989 until 1994 Dave, Lynne, and J.B. ran Uncle Dave's. Dave and Lynne worked in the headquarters in Vermont, and J.B. lived and worked in Boston, commuting to Vermont two to three days each week. After the early days, when everyone did everything, the responsibilities were doled out according to ability and preference: Lynne ran production, product development, and employee relations; Dave and J.B. worked on sales, marketing, and finance.

But adding a son to the dynamics of a couple in business proved overwhelming. They often found themselves at a standstill, emotions clouding day-to-day business situations. Their relationships as well as the business were suffering. They found a therapist to help them.

"She mediated discussions among the three of us. With her help we were able to work through and control our emotions in order to deal with business decisions in a fact-based, logical manner," said J.B. "She was great. Without her we would have had real, lasting trouble. "

In 1994, J.B. left the company to get his MBA at Harvard Business School.

"It was hard when J.B. left.," said Dave. "I understood as a father why J.B. wanted and felt he needed to leave, and I supported his wanting to further his education. But as a business partner, I wasn't happy. We lost a valuable asset."

"And," Lynne added, "at the same time two other key employees gave their notices: the head of our distribution division and our bookkeeper. It was a tough six-month transition."

Will you let your children come work with you? What if this becomes a problem? What if the business is adversely affecting your relationship as a couple? Will you sacrifice your business in order to save your marriage? If your marriage fails, what will become of the business? If the business fails, what will become of the marriage?

These are not the easiest questions to consider when deciding to open a business, but they may become important to answer in the course of running your enterprise. In any job situation there will be conflict. But when the business is also a family, how the conflict may or may not be resolved has far-reaching consequences.

One of the most difficult tasks a couple in business will face is how to separate emotions from fact-based decision-making. Family members have firmly rooted patterns of behavior. Be it a couple or a couple and extended family, these patterns will appear in the business arena. It will be of utmost importance to illuminate them and decide whether they are helpful or harmful in decision making and communication. There are ways to make them more constructive by rooting out the destructive aspects. This is an important task that needs to be addressed, one that will probably be hammered out one decision after another as the business unfolds.

Zippy Gazpacho

The product that was the most fun to develop at Uncle Dave's was the Bloody Mary Fixin's. (Hereafter known as Zippy Fixin's.) After countless Bloody Mary brunches, they realized they had to omit the vodka in order to get some unslurred critiques for the final blend.

Once finding the perfect mixture, they tried some Zippy Fixin's in a Gazpacho recipe. (But don't be afraid to add vodka for a zippy brunch.) This can be prepared a day ahead.

4 cups tomato juice

1 small onion, minced

1 clove of garlic, minced

2 tablespoons olive oil

2 tablespoons red wine or balsamic vinegar

1 teaspoon honey

1 lemon for lemon juice, fresh

1 generous tablespoon Zippy Fixin's

1 diced cucumber

2 scallions, diced

8 fresh tomatoes, peeled, seeded and diced

1 green or red pepper, diced

1/4 cup parsley, chopped

Combine all ingredients and chill for 2 hours. If desired, puree last 5 items. You can also vary the recipe with vegetable substitutes such as chopped celery, carrots, broccoli or sugarsnap peas.

Makes 16 Servings

5

Your Employees Are Your Business

The finest planning or richness of funds, the best idea or smartest sales pitch will not run your company. It is the elbow grease you and your employees apply that makes it all come together. Whom you hire and how you manage your employees will set the tone of your daily work. How your employees feel about their work will become evident to your customers and suppliers. How they treat your customers and suppliers will be a direct indication of how you treat your customers and suppliers. You set the stage.

When is it time to hire? What qualities do you look for in an employee? Do you need an employee handbook? How does a couple present themselves to their staff? Do you want to hire your family? How do you turn over to someone else tasks that you have been doing yourself? Hiring an employee should never be taken lightly, no matter what the job description.

Managing is a skill that is learned. It is a combination of

compassion, clarity of task, listening skills, and the ability to me-
diate, create boundaries, and hold the line. It is knowing how to
let other people do their jobs and letting them make their own
mistakes. As a manager you need to keep your eye on the big
picture even while immersed in the day-to-day, minute-by-
minute functions that a small business demands of its owners. It
is important to know your own strengths and weaknesses in order
to be able to see them in others. It is an asset if either spouse has
had managerial experience that included hiring. If not, you'll be
learning by doing. Research hiring policies and legal issues. Try
not to hire under the gun. Employees leave legacies, positive and
negative.

Traits of a Good Worker

Good sense of self

Enthusiasm

Good communication skills

Ability to take direction

Responsible

Interest in job

Desire to learn

Willing to grow

When Is It Time to Hire?

A couple-owned business is lucky. It has two employees right
from the get-go, which is the number of employees that eight of
the companies profiled in this book had at the start. The two

exceptions are The Herb Patch, which was a running business with employees when Diane and Richard bought the company, and Mother Myrick's, a retail operation that needed staff from day one. The remaining eight companies were run by the couples, with volunteer help from their family and friends. When is it time to hire?

"We hired our first employee when we were working seven days a week, day and night, and we couldn't get the work done," said Harry Haff from Yesterday's Kitchen.

Whenever the time comes, prepare. Write a job description. Educate yourself about the legal aspects of being an employer. Know what it is you'll expect from that person. Let them know what they can expect from you.

The first employee hired at Uncle Dave's had been working at a convenience store.

"Our daughter Andrea found her," said Lynne. "Margaret was our first bookkeeper. When you are first starting out, your first hire has the advantage of starting at the ground level with you. The good part about this is that they are usually pretty confident about their future with you, and you get a lot of their energy. They become almost as invested as you are in growing the business. On the downside, you may be looking for guidance from someone who doesn't have any more experience than you do. You may be setting up procedures and precedents that aren't the best for the company."

Running a business in a rural location has its own unique challenges. There are just not as many people in the hiring pool. Lynne and Dave had to hire inexperienced help even though neither of them had the experience in certain departments to be able to train them. How far away an employee lives can also be a problem.

"No matter how much they want the job, I won't hire them if they live more than twenty or thirty miles away. They're just not going to be able to get to work if there is a blizzard," Lynne said.

Over the past eight years, twenty employees have passed through the doors of Uncle Dave's. Most of the employees have found Uncle Dave's through local want ads, although word of mouth and the Employment Office of Vermont have provided some candidates. Today there are six people who work in the office, including Lynne and Dave.

One year after being in business, Lynne drafted one of their staff, Margaret, to interview the potential candidates.

"Margaret would interview someone and tell him or her a little about us and what our personalities were and what it would be like to work for us. As an employee, Margaret could give them some real information. In turn, she would tell us whether she thought they were qualified and if they would be a good fit for us," explained Lynne. "A third party can ask some questions and share some information that we just can't. It is a great tool.

"It is important for employees to understand that when they come to work for a couple, especially in the early years of growing a business, there may be more stress than in a business without the dynamics of married partners.

"I think that because you are a family business, people know that they are going to hear some yelling or see some kissing. But we are both pretty good about not dragging them into professional or personal differences. We never make an employee take sides. But, because we are a small staff with a small office, everyone knows what the argument is about. There is no privacy. Many times we're logical enough and reasonable enough to wait until everybody has gone home to air these hot issues. Usually no one gets hurt.

"I think that employees, after a certain amount of time, become perceptive about who they go to for what kind of issue. They'll say to me, 'Before I have to tell Dave this, what do you think is the best way for me to approach him?'

"In a couple, the one who has the most patience and is the least reactive is the one who employees will go to first. Dave and I have had a lot of discussions about the employees' performance. Dave is very determined and has set expectations. He has less patience than I do. I am slower to make decisions and judgments. Our styles sometimes clash. When he is saying 'This should be done today,' I say, 'Wait until tomorrow.' Sometimes I'm right, sometimes he's right. But in the employees' eyes, the one who is the most patient is always right."

Dave and Lynne have written an employee manual. They worked with Norbert Johnston, a business consultant, who used software called *The Employee Manual Maker* (see Appendix). They also borrowed employee manuals from other companies to help them make sure theirs was complete.

A handbook not only outlines the benefits and policies directly affecting employees, it also details the company's philosophy and the way the company operates. Having a handbook gives potential employees key information that they need and that you would otherwise have to explain to them. It outlines your expectations and rights as an employer and explains to them in writing what they can expect from you.

Building Layers of Management

As a company grows, its needs to change. When a company is small, the employers and employees work side by side. There is no need for middle management. What happens when the busi-

What's In an Employee Handbook?

An Overview of the Company
  Background
  Mission statement
  Company beliefs
  Organizational chart
  Key players
Employment
  Employment Classifications
    Full-time employees
    Part-time employees
  Employment Policies
    Anniversary date
    Business hours
    Introductory period
    Outside employment, etc.
Compensation and Performance
  Wages and Salary Policies
    Pay period and hours
    Time cards/Records
    Deductions, etc.
  Work Schedule
    Business hours
    Attendance and tardiness policies
    Lunch break, etc.
  Benefits
    Vacation days
    Holidays
    The benefit package
      Eligibility

(continued)

> Paid leaves of absence
> Unpaid leaves of absence
> Insurance coverage, etc.
> *Other Policies*
>   Discounting
>   Dress code
>   Expense reimbursements
>   Grievances
>   Layoff and recall
>   Safety
>   Use of company vehicle, etc.

ness grows to a point when it is necessary to have other managers besides the owners? Is the owner ready to delegate some of their responsibility? Can those managers come from within, or will they need to be hired from the outside? This is a critical point in the growth of a business. The decisions made affect the lives of the people who work for the company. Running a large company with departments and a large payroll creates complexities that a company with a few employees doesn't have.

We had outgrown all our collective knowledge

When Jonathan and Carol from Putney Pasta started their company, they had their hands in everything. They worked closely with their employees in all aspects of their business. Information flowed from customer to employee to owner. By the time they had outgrown their old plant, they had eighteen employees and were running three shifts. Carol shared these observations and experiences:

"When we moved to our new building seventeen out of eighteen employees came with us. We have a core group that has been with us since we were three years in business. We've been through divorces, weddings, and babies. As the business was growing, there was a lot of contact. Now that there are two different buildings and three shifts, that is just not possible. We don't see everyone every day as we used to.

"It became apparent in the first six months that what worked in our smaller plant would not work here. We had outgrown all our collective knowledge. There was ten times the amount of space. Ten times more to be done. The machines were ten times as large. The move made us all feel inept at what we were doing.

"It was killing me trying to hold it all together. When the business was a few steps from the back door, I could easily touch base with every shift. Now I was leaving the house at three in the morning to see the third shift. Jon asked me if I was having an affair with a farmer. I was coming home long after the cows had gone in. Every department from accounting to sales to manufacturing was growing so fast. Our payroll was approaching forty people. It felt like all of a sudden we had put on this huge pair of shoes and that we couldn't walk in them.

"I was used to being involved in everything. I was ready to drop from exhaustion when I came to a realization that if I wanted to micromanage, I would have to stay a small company. It was an eye-opener.

"People used to worry about my ability to let go and delegate. And there was a point, in all honesty, when I didn't know if I had the ability to continue to be president of the company and do it well. I realized that if I didn't let go that I would be stunting the company's growth. We *had* to hire managers to manage the separate departments.

"Initially it was frightening for me to let someone else into our company. I worried that they wouldn't treat the employees with the same dignity and respect that had become protocol for this company. I've learned that if I am confident of an employee's experience, and believe their work philosophy complements ours, then I can trust them enough to let go. We still control the direction of the company. We didn't give up control; we gave up tasks.

"We started in the manufacturing plant. We hired a manager with over twenty-five years experience. It has been incredible. He brought to us knowledge we couldn't have had. I am seeing such incredible growth in old-time employees. They have a mentor now.

"We are becoming a totally different company, but trying hard not to lose that small-company feeling about us.

"Our next goal is to get our employees to start thinking like owners, acting like owners, taking ownership. I want to teach them about business in general and about our business in particular. You can't expect people to really care unless you can show them how their caring about efficiency, inventory, control, waste, etc., can affect the bottom line and the success of the business."

The Attitude of Employees Comes from the Top

The attitude of the owner is reflected in every employee. If the owner is shy and reclusive, this trait will be communicated to the customer. If the owner acts bothered by a customer's request, employees will learn that it is acceptable to show irritation. Even how much an owner uses words like *thank you* and *please* will trickle down to every employee.

Many owners of companies do not recognize how much their behavior affects the interaction between their employees and customers. It is the owners who set the example, whether they like it or not.

The staff of Cold Hollow Cider Mill are friendly and helpful

Francine and Eric Chittenden from Cold Hollow Cider Mill both like working in the store and understand the value of good salesmanship. Even before you meet them, you can see their attitude reflected in the way that each salesperson greets the customers. At Cold Hollow Cider Mill, the salesperson is happy to see you, to answer your question, or to find a product.

When a tour bus drives into the parking lot, the entire staff is alerted immediately. Someone runs out to meet, greet, and welcome the tour group. If Eric is in the shop, he greets the busloads of English-speaking customers. If Francine is there, she welcomes the buses from Canada and their French-speaking customers. If neither is there, then one of the staff does the job. Eric and Francine don't ask anyone to do anything that they don't do themselves, and the Chittendens will do anything.

The staff is helpful and courteous, but they are not high-pressure salespeople. Customers are not an inconvenience to the staff, to be hurried and gotten rid of. Customers can wander around the renovated barn and taste the numerous samples that are always available. But if a customer is looking for help, he or she doesn't have to look far.

This behavior translates into sales.

As Cold Hollow Cider Mill grew to between twenty-five and fifty people, depending on the season, so did the necessary levels of management. The business has been divided into divisions: Production, Delivery, Mail/Order and Bakery/Retail, with a retail manager to run the store.

Oatmeal Cider Jelly Cookies

Making these cookies is the next best thing to being in Vermont and buying them warm with some fresh cider. The Cold Hollow Cider Jelly gives these cookies an unexpected tartness that is a real treat.

1/4 pound (1 stick) margarine, at room temperature

1/4 pound (1 stick) butter, at room temperature

1/2 cup pure maple syrup

1 tablespoon Cold Hollow Cider Jelly, plus 1 cup

1 egg

2 cups whole-wheat pastry flour

1 cup rolled oats

3/4 tablespoon cinnamon

1 teaspoon baking powder

1/2 teaspoon baking soda

1. Preheat oven to 350 degrees.

2. Cream the margarine, butter, maple syrup, one tablespoon of Cold Hollow Cider Jelly, and egg together in a large bowl.

3. In a separate bowl mix the whole-wheat flour, rolled oats, cinnamon, baking powder and baking soda. Add to the butter mixture. Blend thoroughly.

4. Gather the dough in a ball, wrap in waxed paper and refrigerate 4 to 6 hours.

5. Remove the dough from the refrigerator and allow it to soften slightly, about 1 hour.

6. Form the dough into 2-inch balls and place on a dry cookie sheet. Flatten slightly and indent dough ball with thumb. Fill each indentation with 1 teaspoon of Cold Hollow Cider Jelly.

7. Bake 17 to 20 minutes, until brown. Additional jelly may be added to the center of cookie after baking, if desired.

Makes 2 dozen (2 1/2 inch) cookies

Being a couple in business introduces a unique dynamic that affects relationships with employees. Carol Berry from Putney Pasta expressed the fact that she and Jonathan consider their role in their company as being somewhat parental. The nurturing and security that a parent offers a child can be an asset in employer-employee relationships. But the need for every child to grow up and rebel against his or her parents in the process may become a problem if the employee has not fully matured. This may bring up behaviors in the employee that have more to do with their parents than with their employers.

The couples in this book have had to learn to refrain from arguing in front of their employees. They will tell you that that is a good thing. No child likes to hear his or her parents argue excessively. And, it's almost unavoidable that a couple as owners will be seen as parental figures.

Not only does the couple in business need to address all the same issues that any other business owner does but they must also be aware of the dynamics of their own relationship. Remembering this when dealing with employees may shed some light on a situation that is baffling you.

6

When to Get Help

Every Business Needs Outside Help

Help comes in all forms. And the truth is, a business needs help from day one and never stops needing outside support. The first words of advice anyone in business will give you are—ask for help.

Often help comes in the form of education. What are the elements of starting a business? How do you find money? What is a business plan? Once the business.is up and running you will need different kinds of help—help with marketing, management issues, or financial concerns. As a business grows, it will change. What looked correct on paper may not materialize in the marketplace. The business may need the owners to change their ways of managing. Sales may be flat. Often an outside person will see something that you cannot see. It is common practice in large corporations to hire people from the outside to help solve problems. Anyone involved closely in the day-to-day running of a business will find it hard to be objective. Although you may be the one who is most intimately involved in your business, you can't always be the problem solver.

Are you open to criticism? Is it easy for you to ask for help? What happens if somebody tells you that you are wrong? Can you change? Look back in your life at times when you have had to change. How did you respond? Is *change* a dirty word in your vocabulary? All the couples in this book have needed help of one kind or another at one time or another.

Ron and Jacki sought a management consultant to help them change

In 1985, two years after Mother Myrick's major expansion, Jacki hired a management consultant.

Sales had increased to close to $400,000 a year. Ron and Jacki had executed the design that they had proposed in their business plan and had successfully added a bakery to the existing ice cream and candy shop.

The vision that Jacki and Ron had for the bakery was a place where people would come and have a cup of coffee with a slice of cake. But what was happening was that customers wanted to buy whole cakes. This demand increased the level of production that was needed from baking one or two cakes at a time to baking many. The bakery needed more space, equipment, and overall organization. Recipes had to be adapted to increase batch size. Jacki and Ron thought that if they hired more help to work under their baker, Tom, the bakery would be able to meet the demand. But Tom had no management experience. Jacki, Ron, and Tom were becoming increasingly frustrated because their best efforts were not helping the department. Tom didn't know how to manage, Ron couldn't get Tom to do what needed to be done, and Jacki couldn't figure out how to help.

Jacki was a charter member of the Woman Business Owner Network of Vermont. The organization, created in 1980, provided an arena for women business owners to network with one another. The organization held regular meetings where topics like finance issues, expansion, employees, and personal balance were presented and discussed.

It was through the Woman Business Owner Network that Jacki met a human-resources consultant whom she hired to work with Mother Myrick's.

Jacki and Ron worked with the consultant extensively for three years, more in the slow season and less in the busy season. Ron and Jacki also participated in a forum with four other couples in business in Manchester that met weekly for six months.

Jacki and Ron embrace a team-based approach to quality improvement and management called Total Quality Management (TQM), developed by Dr. W. Edwards Deming. Ron and Jacki tested the team-based management style in the bakery. The bakery staff became a team. The team discussed problems and came up with solutions. A member was elected to be in charge of a particular aspect of the running of the department. The team did performance appraisals, scheduling, quality control, etc. Upon implementing the team approach, the bakery became more organized, and production and morale increased.

From there Jacki and Ron worked with the consultant on their own management style.

"I was set in my ways in terms of how to be a manager," Ron said. "I knew what I wanted and wanted it done *my* way. But it wasn't working. I was frustrated and disappointed. I didn't think anyone cared about their jobs. Jacki had been trying to help me, but neither of us had any other management experience. By seeking help, we learned how to change ourselves so we could be more effective leaders—coaches, really.

"I began to see things differently. I became sensitive to the needs of others—that their personal problems were, at times, more important than a work problem. I came to understand that the staff was trying their best, that they did care. We have a lot of people who have been with us a long time. I began to accept that others might have a method that was better than mine.

"My job had changed since I started making fudge. I needed to become a better manager. I needed to provide others with tools for success, to make sure they had everything they needed to do the best job they could—from tools to physical help and if they needed it to emotional support."

At the same time, Ron and Jacki embraced an internal customer concept which changed the culture of the shop. The concept is that everyone who works at Mother Myrick's is in service to someone else who is in service to the customer.

"I am in service to the staff to make sure they have all that they need in order to get their work done," Ron said.

Morale improved tremendously and has continued to do so. So much so that when both the Bakery Team Leader and the Candy Team Leader decided to get pregnant, they timed it so they would have their babies in between seasons and be back to work when most needed. That's teamwork!

In their new culture, Ron and Jacki have tried to make room for other employees to have a say in the direction of the company.

"We explained the difference between an idea and a command," Jacki said. "An idea is just an idea, not an ultimatum. When we have meetings Ron and I use different color pens on the agenda. If I use the color that represents boss, that represents veto power. The idea in this color must be done. The other color represents us as team members who have equal status with every other member. These points are up for discussion. The relationships in team building are always fragile. It's hard, perhaps impossible, for them to look at us as anything else but bosses."

The consultant also helped Ron and Jacki articulate their vision and formulate a mission statement.

"Our mission statement and vision are very important to us. This statement describes the way we do business and *wanted* to continue to do business, but we needed help to articulate it," explained Jacki. "Either in the interview process with a new employee, or in the early stages of orientation, we discuss the details, discuss the wisdom, and explain how we implement our way of doing business."

"We still get help on a need basis," Jacki said. "It is so important. We have used other consultants for graphics, marketing, and mail order. We belong to the *Direct Marketing Association*, and the *Industry Organization of Retail Confections*. We meet people who can relate to our level of expertise, and also those we can learn from. We have local friends who are couples in business. We can cry on each other's shoulders, or get advice on how they are doing something."

Jacki has always been open to looking for people outside Mother Myrick's who can add to her knowledge. Besides having other ideas and solutions, a third party can alleviate pressure that may be building between spouses. By consulting outsiders, both Jacki and Ron have someone else to turn to for help. As a couple in business, hiring a consultant helps them to separate the stress and conflict of the business from their relationship.

True to their mission statement, Ron and Jacki are also very involved in civic organizations and community relations. They sponsor the Vermont Committee Against Breast Cancer. Jacki has developed a summer reading program and has run it since 1989. She is also on the board of the Vermont Reading Partners,

Mother Myrick's Beliefs

We believe that in order to be successful, we must satisfy three constituencies: our employees, our customers, and our community. We must strive to attain the highest level of ethical and social standards in this endeavor. The goals, policies, and activities of the company reflect our commitment to these principles as well as our determination to remain responsive to the needs of our constituents.

Employees: We believe that the personal and professional growth of our employees and of our business to the full potential of each are inextricably bound together. This growth can best take place in an atmosphere of mutual trust, frankness, cooperation, and encouragement. We want our employees to feel good about themselves and Mother Myrick's because we believe that people who feel good about themselves live their lives and produce results that benefit the individual, the business, and our society.

Customers: We believe that we must understand and exceed the expectations of our customers for confectionery products and services for their life celebrations, large and small. This is accomplished in an atmosphere of unconditional service, and genuine care and concern for their satisfaction.

(continued)

an adult-literacy program. In the shop, Jacki has established Easter egg contests, an Easter parade, and an Easter bonnet workshop. The candy kitchen hosts classes and schools.

Ron is a member of the town's Transportation Initiative Committee, a past president of the Chamber of Commerce, and is on the Planning Commission for the town. He is also an appointed member of the Governor's Commission of Travel and Tourism. Ron has also been a guest lecturer in the MBA program at the University of Connecticut.

Our Community: We believe that our community is a vital part of our extended family. Our company is committed to dedicating its resources to enhance the quality of life of everyone we touch by developing programs that foster personal growth and encourage participation in life's celebration. This effort is extended to other companies as well as individual citizens.

Our mission is to be a profitable, well-managed maker of fine chocolates, baked goods, and fountain desserts for our retail and mail-order customers, providing them with the highest value in affordable luxury for their personal celebrations.

We achieve this through uncompromising service, attention to detail, quality ingredients and methods, cleanliness, product presentation, and unconditional satisfaction in an atmosphere where we are hosts and customers are our guests at life's party.

Mother Myrick's, as a company, nurtures team spirit and holds each employee in their highest possibilities. We carry this commitment and regard for the individual into our community. We share and contribute our energy, ideas, and spirit to the community as a whole.

Our goal is to have our name be synonymous with "the best."

Don't Underestimate the Power of Stress

One of the most stressful aspects of owning your own business is that all the responsibility for the company falls on your shoulders. The people with whom you do business, your customers, your employees, and your family are depending on you to follow through. Most small-business owners will confess that they are almost never completely away from their business, even on a tropical island vacation.

Stress accumulates. On the one hand, a couple has it easier than the individual who owns a business and comes home at night

Doc's Demise

*In 1979, the woman who introduced Ron and Jacki,
Susanella, invited her Aunt Lucy to Vermont to celebrate her 80th
birthday. She brought her own birthday cake with her, a moist
lemony concoction that was a hit with the crowd.*

*Jacki asked her for the recipe for the shop. Aunt Lucy was
flattered and gladly divulged her secrets. Lemon Lulu found a
home, and is one of the most popular of all desserts served at
Mother Myrick's. Although Aunt Lucy died at age 91, Lemon Lulu
shows up at every party.*

*It isn't the recipe for Lemon Lulu you'll find below. For the
cake you'll have to call and have one sent to you. Below, you'll find
the undoing of the good old Doc.*

2 thin slices Lemon Lulu Cake

1 scoop vanilla ice cream

4 tablespoons Mother Myrick's Hot Fudge Sauce, heated

4 tablespoons fresh raspberries or sliced strawberries

2 dollops fresh whipped cream

1. Lay the two thin slices of cake facing point-to-point on
an oversized plate.

2. Place the scoop of ice cream in the middle of the slices.

3. Pour the hot fudge over the ice cream.

4. Place the pile of berries on top and finish off with the
freshly whipped cream.

Recipe for 1 Serving (1 cake serves up to 16)

to a spouse who wishes her husband or his wife weren't spending day and night consumed by work. On the other hand, when both are immersed in the business, neither spouse is advocating time away from the business, until one or the other makes it a priority.

Marilyn needed help with stress management techniques

When Marilyn and Harry from Yesterday's Kitchen were two years into their business, Marilyn began to worry about her health and their relationship. As a single parent working for a large corporation she was not unaccustomed to stress, but she had never felt quite like this before. The combination of being newly married and in business with her husband was creating a tremendous amount of anxiety. Marilyn was constantly tense. She and Harry were fighting often.

Marilyn sought help in stress management.

"The therapist helped me see where I had lost sight of the big picture. Harry and I started to talk to each other again about our relationship. All our energies had been going into the business. We began to look at ways to create time in our lives outside our business. Even if it was to get a sandwich and sit outside to eat it, in tiny increments we created some space to have a life. We reminded each other that we respected each other's abilities and respected the abilities of those who worked for us. We both had to be willing to let go of some control."

The therapist worked with Marilyn to develop ways to communicate with Harry that were not destructive. The yelling and screaming weren't working.

"We now agree to listen before interrupting and totally disagreeing," Marilyn said. "Strangely enough this works pretty well. And I think we managed to get past pretending to listen while thinking, yeah, yeah, yeah."

At first when Marilyn started to leave in the middle of the afternoon to take a walk to the pond, Harry would look up from his work and tell her to have fun. When she continued to leave, he started to get irritated. This didn't stop Marilyn. Then she began to pack a picnic lunch. Soon, he wanted to go, too.

Little by little they brought some balance back into their lives. Five years and hundreds of gallons of olive oil later, they are remembering to have some fun, to show respect for each other, and to appreciate each other.

"I believe our marriage is stronger from being in business together," Marilyn said.

Networking with Other Business Owners

All ten couples in this book know one another. They have met over the years while doing business as part of the Vermont Specialty Food Association.

What makes this group so interesting is that they are competitors. Sometimes it gets fierce between them. There have also been some close friendships made among the couples.

"Our only friends are in the specialty food industry, especially couples," said Richard Copley, from The Herb Patch. "Who else can understand us? Who else do we have time to see?"

Other couples understand the hardships and highlights of being in business together. Couples in business can end each other's sentences. Somewhere with this kind of shared knowledge, emotional loads are lightened. Situations that seem catastrophic when it's just the two of you dealing with them take on a new complexion when you realize that these are challenges suffered and survived by most couples in business together. Whether it's others in similar businesses or not, sharing knowledge and experiences can only help you all.

Help Available for the Couple in Business (That the Couple in Business Might Not Even Know They Need)

Business Help

U.S. Department of Commerce—See Appendix

    Minority Business Development Agency

Small Business Administration (SBA)—See Appendix

    Small Business Institutes (SBI)

    University Business Development Centers (UBDC)

Service Corps of Retired Executives (SCORE)—See Appendix

State government

Chamber of Commerce

Community business people—Ask advice

Business people in your industry—Ask advice

Bankers, lawyers, accountants

Advertising firms

Associations: general or specialized business and professional organizations; gender specific, minority, special interest—even religious groups

Businesses run by couples

Businesses in same industry as yours

Customers—Your customers can be your best source of information and advice

Suppliers

Consultants: human resources, marketing and sales, financial, graphic/design

Seminars and trade shows

Libraries

Trade magazines

(continued)

Relationship/Personal Help

    Marriage counselors

    Stress-management counselors

    Men's service or social organizations

    Women's service, social, and support groups

    Friends

    Other couples in business

Harry's Famous Apple Cranberry Tart

Harry Haff created this recipe one night when company was coming and there was no dessert in the house.

1 10-inch pie shell, prepared or made from scratch

1/4 cup cinnamon and sugar mixture (2/3 sugar to 1/3 cinnamon) or granulated maple sugar

1 9-ounce jar Vermont Garden Crazy Cranberry Relish

4 large tart apples, peeled, cored and thinly sliced

2 tablespoons maple syrup

1 teaspoon cinnamon

1. Preheat oven to 400 degrees.

2. Roll pie dough to fit an ungreased 10-inch tart pan with removable bottom. Fold edges over 1/2 inch above top of rim.

3. Sprinkle the bottom with the cinnamon and sugar mixture or granulated maple sugar.

4. Spread the Vermont Garden Crazy Cranberry Relish over the layer of sugar.

5. Arrange the apple slices in a circular fan shape on top of the relish. Drizzle with the maple syrup and lightly dust with the cinnamon.

6. Bake about 30 to 40 minutes. Serve with vanilla ice cream.

Serves 8

7

Sales and Marketing

The couples profiled in this book have had to do a lot more than make a fine-tasting apple cider jelly, raspberry hot cocoa, or spicy Caribbean barbecue sauce to succeed. They have had to develop marketing strategies and sales methods to best promote their companies and products.

A marketing strategy can be defined as an overall plan for promoting the image of a company and creating and feeding a demand for its products. An effective strategy will need to define the company's customers and their potential buying power. Pricing policy needs to be implemented; advertising and promotional logistics decided upon.

When a decision is made to open a business, there has been a determination made that there is enough of a demand for the product that the company is going to sell, or that the product is something that does not exist and will fill a niche. Putney Pasta took a chance that there would be a market for a vegetable-filled pasta. There was. Uncle Dave's and Jasmine & Bread both introduced an all-natural ketchup as an alternative to Heinz's, which has dominated the market so completely that for many people the flavor of ketchup is the flavor of Heinz. The alternative ketchups of both companies have had minimal success. Mother Myrick's rode the wave of America's sweet tooth—from chocolate to ice cream to fine pastries. Their timing was perfect.

To make appropriate decisions on where to put your marketing efforts, and dollars, there are innumerable questions that need to be answered. Who are your customers? How do you find customers? How do you get more? What do your customers think of your products? What do you want them to think of your products? How can you capitalize on your existing products? What is your company's image? Where do you advertise? What is your sales policy? How do you price your products? What is your competition doing? How big a slice of the market pie do you need to stay in business and to grow?

The Importance of Image

Part of the success of all the businesses found in this book can be attributed to their association with the locale. Vermont, with a reputation of a quality of life that includes good, farm-fresh food and a slower pace than that of most of the country, lends a unique cachet to these specialty food producers.

Yet each company has developed its own image. Sherrie Maurer, from Jasmine & Bread, embraced the concept of earth mother in order to present her product line as an all-natural line made with a mother's love. The name Mother Myrick's was decided upon for a similar reason. Yesterday's Kitchen conjures up nostalgia for a time more innocent than ours.

"Be careful how you pick your name," said Diane Copley from The Herb Patch. "We bought ours. But as we began to expand, it became a hindrance. How can you connote hot cocoa and herbs? The tastes just don't blend."

Most of these companies have appealed to their customers through the use of homey, old-fashioned images. In the food business enticing people's senses is good business.

Are you really Uncle Dave?

"Are you really Uncle Dave?" the man asked Dave Lyon. Dave is dressed in product costume, blue jean overalls and red-and-black plaid flannel shirt and hat.

"I sure am," Dave responded, sticking his thumbs through his suspenders and strutting around the front of the booth at the Vermont Specialty Food Show in Burlington, giving the man the famous Dave smile. It's the same smile that is caricatured on the labels of all the products that Uncle Dave's produces. Uncle Dave is the Aunt Jemima of specialty foods.

Lynne Andreen, dressed in a sunflower dress and a straw hat with her blond hair tied back, promotes their new product, Sunflower Pesto. She stands in the booth, smiling as she watches her husband in action. Behind Lynne hangs a fifteen-foot quilt she made depicting Uncle Dave's. It is a country scene with a blue Vermont sky, tall trees, and a winding dirt road with a covered bridge. The Uncle Dave's building is in the center, and Uncle Dave is driving a truck filled to the brim with tomatoes.

"Uncle Dave's image is that of a farmer who goes out in the fields and plucks the tomatoes for his company's sauces," Lynne explained. "With the outfit Uncle Dave wears he stands out at all the shows and meetings. He is a personality."

Uncle Dave's has created a strong product identification.

Their packaging stands out as Dave does in his farmer's garb. Uncle Dave's creates a personal relationship with the customer and reinforces the image of a small, caring company, a company that a customer can feel good about.

Each Sale Is the Most Important Sale

Small companies don't have large budgets for marketing. Yet promoting the company is what is going to bring in more sales. Deciding on whether to advertise or how to promote a business takes some thought. How can you best reach your customers? What kind of advertising can you afford? How can you reach the most people with the least amount of dollars?

Ward's Pond Farm, Jasmine & Bread and Yesterday's Kitchen have garnered many customers at farmers' markets. Customer by customer their lists have grown. Some of those customers who bought only one or two bottles at first have turned into big customers, using their products as corporate gifts, ordering a hundred or more at a time. You never know who is buying your product. Don't pigeonhole people. Ask each customer where they live, what line of work they are in. There could be a big market behind a modest smile. The most basic form of advertising is word of mouth. A happy customer is your best sales tool—a happy customer is ultimately your only sales tool.

Jonathan Rutstein from Bread & Chocolate had a chance every retailer dreams of—selling on QVC, a television shopping network. Tens of thousands of customers watched Jonathan talk about his product. He sold 16,000 tins of hot chocolate.

Guerilla marketing

Sherrie Maurer grew up in an inner-city housing project. The street smarts she acquired in her early years have helped her in creating her business strategies.

"There is book knowledge or schooling on how to run a business. Then there are street smarts. You run things by your gut feeling. You're always thinking about what you are going to do and what somebody else might do—how to protect yourself and go after what you want. When you're on the streets you're always aware of what's going on in every corner. That's the only way you survive. You're aware of what the person in front of you is doing, the person behind you, on the side and everywhere else. And you are continually adjusting your position by what your antennae are telling you is happening.

"My mind is always going a mile a minute. What if I step this way, what if I step forward or what if I step backward? What will the repercussions be and how will I land on my feet? How can I get this done with no money? How can I get the advice I need without having to pay for it?"

Sherrie discovered early that *she* could sell her product better than anyone else could. Equipped with only their Beyond Word Catsup, a few plain crackers, and a spoon, she and Hugh marketed their product by canvassing Vermont. Hugh drove and Sherrie sold. Village stores and markets liked what they tasted and ordered. One by one, the accounts began to accumulate.

The Maurers discovered the weekend craft fair and joined the circuit. In the early days Sherrie stayed up all night producing product while Hugh slept. Then they packed up their van, and Sherrie slept while Hugh drove.

Between their driving around Vermont and doing many

country fairs Sherrie and Hugh built a small customer base. But they needed to sell to the big guys. They decided to ambush Bloomingdale's. Most companies, if attempting to sell to a major department store, will send a letter, samples, and try to set up an appointment with a buyer. Sherrie and Hugh had other plans.

They sent some friends into the gourmet food section at the Bloomingdale's in New York City to ask if they carried Jasmine & Bread products. When the salesclerk said no, the couple raved about the product and left. A few weeks later Sherrie and Hugh hit the city. One morning Hugh went to the store and asked for Jasmine & Bread products. Once again, the answer was no.

The next afternoon Sherrie popped into Bloomingdale's with her catsup, a basket of spoons, and a box of crackers. The buyers tasted and bought, pleased to have a product that so many "customers" had requested.

Sherrie and Hugh have perfected another guerrilla technique: they use their customers as sales representatives. When customers call to ask where they can get Jasmine & Bread products in their area, Sherrie sends them samples to bring to their local gourmet food shop, and gives them a jar or two for their effort.

Part of the fun of business is making the sale. Be creative.

Think Big, Act Bigger

Every business was once small. The ones who make it big are the ones who are not afraid to take a chance. Make that phone call— What have you got to lose?

After reading an article in *Forbes* magazine about how Absolut Vodka likes to help young businesses, Dave and J. B. Lyon from Uncle Dave's devised a plan. J.B. called the company with the idea that Absolut and Uncle Dave's do a promotion together—

Super Spiced Shrimp

Sherrie Maurer has a knack for the hot and spicy. These will keep
you on your toes!

1/2 cup White Lightning prepared horseradish

1/3 cup olive oil

1/4 cup Worcestershire sauce

1/2 cup Caribbean Heat Sauce

2 quarts water

1 12-ounce bottle of amber beer

5 small dried chilies (like Chile de arbol), optional

8 large cloves of garlic, peeled

1 teaspoon yellow mustard seed

4 bay leaves

2 pounds raw, medium shrimp, peeled and deveined,
leaving
tail shell intact

1 large lemon, thinly sliced

1 tablespoon salt

1. Whisk White Lightning horseradish, olive oil, Worcestershire sauce and Caribbean Heat to blend in a bowl and cover.
(Can be prepared 8 hours ahead.) Use at room temperature.

2. In a large, heavy saucepan over high heat, bring water,
beer, chilies, garlic, mustard seeds and bay leaves to a boil. Reduce
heat to medium and simmer, covered, for 10 minutes.

3. Add shrimp, lemon and salt to pot. Simmer until shrimp
are just cooked through, about 3 minutes. Pour shrimp mixture
through large strainer, discarding liquids. Transfer contents of
strainer to large bowl.

4. Add the horseradish mixture and stir to blend. Cool to
room temperature, about 30 minutes.

5. Place a big bowl of the shrimp in the middle of the table
and give everyone an ice-cold beer, a small plate for discarded
shells, and a pile of hot, damp towels.

Makes 8 Servings

with Uncle Dave's Bloody Mary Mix and Absolut Vodka—the Absolut Best Bloody Mary. Absolut like the idea, and they made a deal. Absolut ordered from them thousands of little packages of Uncle Dave's Bloody Mary mix, which they affixed to bottles of Absolut Vodka. Absolut and Uncle Dave's did joint advertising. It was a big break for Uncle Dave's.

In order to capitalize on the sale, Dave, J.B., and Lynne decided to host a party to create the World's Largest Bloody Mary. At a popular bar in downtown Boston, they built a fiberglass mug that would hold 300 gallons of Welch's tomato juice, 50 gallons of Absolut vodka, and 40 pounds of Uncle Dave's Bloody Mary Mix. Two thousand guests came to drink, and Uncle Dave's used the opportunity to introduce three new pasta sauces.

J.B. sent out press releases to the local radio, television, and newspapers, who are always looking for a good story. And because Uncle Dave's partner in this event was a recognized brand, they got lots of pickup in the national media as well.

It was the event that generated publicity, not merely the introduction of a new product . . . and this was far more effective in promoting Uncle Dave's name and products than any paid-for advertising campaign could have been.

Got anything new?

"One of the first questions our distributors will ask us is 'Got anything new?'" said Diane Copley from The Herb Patch. "In our industry, the gourmet market is always looking for new products. And they are expensive to test, market, and produce."

Diane and Richard try to introduce a new product every year. Their most recent addition is their line of teas packaged in boxes painted by Vermont artists. They prepared a mock-up of the line and presented it at a fancy food show.

"We got a great response and took many orders before starting production. This is the way we introduce new products. We make sure there is a demand before we invest," said Diane.

Ellen and Davis Koier from Ward's Pond Farm learned early to capitalize on their products, to find added value. When producing their smoked nuts, they first roasted them drizzled with maple syrup. Their friends seemed to time their visits so they would arrive exactly when the nuts were between the roasting stage and the smoking stage. Why not sell maple roasted nuts as well as smoked nuts? Why not sell the maple syrup? Also, people loved the unique stoneware jug in which they packaged the maple syrup. Why not sell the stoneware containers too? This ancillary merchandise now comprises 20 percent of their sales.

Marilyn Wedig and Harry Haff from Yesterday's Kitchen package their oils and vinegars in different bottles to appeal to different markets. The Company Collection line is bottled in tall, slender bottles. The labels are printed in an elegant font with names like Oh! Chihuahua Vinegar, Opal Basil Vinegar, and West Indian Oil. These are marketed to the gourmet sophisticate and gift markets. The Vermont Garden line is packaged in smaller, standard-size containers. The labels are brightly colored and easy to read, with names like Mother-in-Law Mustard and Lipsmacking Lemon Relish. These look more "country" to appeal to a different market.

"It's all part of the marketing strategy—what you name your product, how you package it, who you are targeting," said Marilyn Wedig. "We try to hit as much of the market who buy gourmet food products as possible."

As mentioned earlier, both Uncle Dave's and Jasmine & Bread have not had the hoped-for sales of their gourmet ketchup. They both still make the ketchups but learned early on that what you think may sell and people will love is not always the case.

How These Companies Market Their Company and Sell Their Products

Trade shows, fairs and markets

Cold calls

Charity events sponsorship

Paid advertising

Company newsletters for current or potential customers

Personalized customer service: answering all customers' correspondence

An Internet presence with a home page

Network with industry colleagues

Promote to specialty and consumer press through product mailings and information and news releases

Taste testings and other events to introduce new products

Establish effective distribution through wholesalers and distributors

Maintain a retail outlet and/or direct-mail operation

"If we had stayed in ketchup, we would have been out of business a long time ago," said Dave Lyon. "You've got to keep trying. You never know what the public is going to like. Once you find it, ride with it. And then be prepared for that to peter out. In this business, you've got to keep coming out with something new. That's the specialty food business. It's like restaurants. People have their favorites and go back to them all of the time. But they want to try new ones, too."

What you do to market your company and sell your product will evolve as the company does. The company will grow on one success followed by another. What works to sell your product at one point may not at another. What sells today may not tomorrow. As in all areas of business, it is important to be open and adaptable. And if you need help, get it.

8

To Grow or Hold the Line

There are critical moments in the life of a business when owners have to make a decision whether to stay at their present volume of business or to push on to the next stage—whether that means moving from house to office, moving from one building to another, taking on a new product line, or creating a new position.

When is it time to move the business out of the house? Do you want a boutique business, one that is small and managed by just a few? Or a larger business? When is it time to make the leap? As a couple, how driven are you? These are questions that force a couple to examine their position at critical times in the life cycle of their business, to look at where they have come from, where they are now, where they want to go.

Oftentimes the momentum of a business forces a decision. Sometimes life intercedes with its own demands.

When It's Time to Move Out of the House

Nine of these couples have had at least part, if not all, of their businesses in their homes at one time or another. Of the nine, only Sherrie and Hugh Maurer, from Jasmine & Bread currently run their business from home. Two other couples, Marilyn Wedig and Harry Haff, from Yesterday's Kitchen, and Ellen and Davis Koier, from Ward's Pond Farm, have parts of their operation at home. Marilyn has her office in their living room, and Davis smokes and roasts the nuts on their property. The bulk of the work is done in another venue. The other couples have physically separated their businesses from their homes. So when is it time to move out?

The nuts were taking over

Ellen and Davis Koier from Wards Pond Farm did not drastically change their lives when they started their business. In 1987, when they began to make the maple roasted smoked almonds, they were both still teaching. It wasn't until 1989 that Davis left teaching, and it wasn't until 1991, when they incorporated their business, that he took a salary. Ellen has taught full-time, part-time, or not at all—depending on their needs.

The Koiers have had two children since they opened Ward's Pond Farm. Davis, Jr., their eldest child, was three weeks old in 1990 when he went to his first farmers' market with his parents peddling their nuts. Abby, born in 1993, entered the family at the height of their initial business boom, when the business was still in the Koiers' home. They did not move the business out of their home until they were squeezed out.

"Our home gradually surrendered to nuts over the first seven years of our business," said Davis. "By 1993 we felt that the business and family were synonymous. It wasn't as bad as it may sound. The kids weren't in school yet and Ellen had an extremely part-time, flexible teaching arrangement. We could still move to the same rhythm dictated by the business.

"We were manufacturing, packing, and sending fourteen separate products all out of our 150-year-old farmhouse, the kind with small rooms and lots of doors. We filled the mudroom with cartons, totes, jars, and lids. Then we turned the downstairs bedroom into an office/storage room. We lost the kitchen table to the fax machine. We turned a shed into a roasting room. Ward's Pond Farm was steadily taking over the house.

"By 1993 there was one small path from the door through the kitchen and into the living room—which Ellen had declared off-limits to nuts. But by that fall the living room succumbed to a big plywood table on two sawhorses where we pack mail orders.

"By mid-December of 1993 we didn't know which end was up and worried that our children would never be normal growing up this way. We didn't have a clear place to put an order. There was no privacy. Everyone was packing orders everywhere. The phone was ringing constantly. The fax machine was wailing. Somebody was packing nuts three feet from the couch where Ellen was trying to soothe Abby, who had strep throat. We knew it was time to move out.

"We had talked before about moving but had never felt ready to make the jump. We were cautious about the new expense. But not only was our sanity at stake now, we could no longer be efficient in our home.

"We moved the business out of the house in the fall of 1994, to a location close enough that I could walk. Fall is the busiest time of the year. We didn't even have time to unpack, we just hit the ground running in order to fill our Christmas orders. We didn't unpack until February."

Ellen and Davis waited to move out of their home until they had absolutely no space left. Their house was crammed with nuts. The quality of their home life was deteriorating, and the business was suffering. Before making the move from home to commercial space, they had done their research. They waited for the right time and felt they could afford the move.

It is important to consider both the immediate costs of moving and the long-term costs. Study the current market, be realistic about your future projections. Up until their move, Ward's Pond Farm's growth had been steady, growing 20 percent annually. That changed after they moved. The growth in the specialty food market slowed in 1995. Not only had they increased their overhead dramatically, but they also weren't growing as quickly as they had anticipated.

Ellen and Davis compensated by scrutinizing their business, to make it more efficient. During the first seven years in operation, increasing sales was as important as making a profit. All their energy had been focused on making product, to meet the demands of customers in order to pay suppliers. Now they had to find savings inside their operation, become sharper businesspeople. They dissected their business, to learn where they were making money and where they weren't.

"We are so many different businesses," said Davis. "We do manufacturing, shipping, warehousing, mail order, wholesaling, and distributing. We needed to look at each one of those as though they were individual businesses, and to really analyze whether they were making money for us or not. Was something just too expensive to hang on to? Could we find different packaging? Where could we put a little more effort into something in order to maximize our time?

"We looked closely at our mailing list. At that point there were 11,000 names on it. We decided to keep on the list only the people who had placed an order within the last two years or who had been added in those two years. We cut our mailing list in half.

"We made more money sending half out; some of it was from savings on postage and printing. Since then the list has climbed up 17,000 names. We learned the importance of a vital list."

Ellen and Davis have become sharper businesspeople. They weigh every expenditure against what it will earn for them—whether it will enhance their business and their life. They have also decided that they want to stay small.

"We were growing so quickly for a while," said Ellen. "You have to do a lot of everything before you know what is going to work. I don't think either of us wants to be a large company. We like making most of the decisions ourselves and making most of the unique products ourselves. And I don't often see a huge increase in profit just because you get bigger."

Boutique Business

Ellen and Davis have decided to stay small and specialized. They have chosen to keep their business at a level at which they can have balance in their lives, and control in their business. Ellen wants to continue to teach. They both want to be actively involved in raising their children. They like living close to the land. Davis likes being hands-on in his work.

For this couple, to give all their time and energy to a business is not desirable. They have chosen a level of business that fits their lifestyle.

Sherrie and Hugh Maurer have also chosen to stay small.

Smoky Cheese Balls

Ellen and Davis Ward's smoked nuts blend eloquently with cheese. The smoky flavor adds a nice twist to a classic hors d'oeuvre.

1/2 cup cream cheese, room temperature

1/2 cup roquefort cheese, room temperature

2 tablespoons butter, room temperature

1 teaspoon Worcestershire sauce

1 teaspoon paprika

1 dash cayenne pepper

1/2 cups ground Ward's Pond Farm smoked cashews, almonds, pecans, brazil nuts or macadamia nuts.

1. In a large bowl mix together all ingredients except nuts.

2. Shape cheese into 1-inch balls.

3. Spread the nuts out on a dry cookie sheet and roll the cheese balls in the nuts to coat. Place on clean cookie sheet and chill. (You can also make this as one large cheese ball.)

4. Serve with crackers and cut vegetables.

Makes 16 individual balls, or 1 large ball

Their decision was made for them in part because of Sherrie's health.

Health and circumstances kept
this company small

Jasmine & Bread was growing in leaps and bounds in the late 1980s and early 1990s. Being a black woman in a specialty Vermont business had gained Sherrie much publicity. She had articles written about her in the *New York Times, Successful American Entrepreneurs, Women in Business, Black Enterprise, Family Circle, Working Woman,* and the *Wall Street Journal.* "Never say never," was one of her favorite sayings. She had cooked up a business from a few thousand dollars, with determination and support from her husband and family. Sherrie was working day and night, and Hugh was working all the hours around his part-time carpentry jobs. They began to consider moving the operation out of their home. Sherrie was doing her usual street research, talking to anyone and everyone who had more knowledge than she.

The advice was mixed: "Don't move out of your house unless you absolutely have to"; "If you need to raise money and you look to investors, you are letting go of part of the business"; "If you move out, you will have two overheads to support."

Then life threw some curveballs. In 1991, three months after Hugh had been laid off from his job with a building company and their health insurance had lapsed, Sherrie was diagnosed with breast cancer. There was more to endure. Sherrie, Hugh, and their daughter Amber were in a car accident in September of 1992. Sherrie received head injuries which further impaired her. During the next few years while Sherrie was undergoing treatment and recovering, her daughters, Lauree and Amber, along with Hugh kept the business afloat. But with Sherrie unable to work for so long, the business began to lose its momentum. No new products were introduced, no new accounts were brought in, they cut back drastically on the number of shows they attended in order to have more time to help Sherrie recover.

By 1996 Sherrie was four years out of treatment, and her cancer was in remission. The injuries from the car accident had healed. But the experience had changed Sherrie. Although her business life has resumed, she is less frantic, less driven. She sleeps more and tries to get some time away from Jasmine & Bread. *Balance* is now an important word in her vocabulary.

"It took me a long time to trust in tomorrow," Sherrie said. "I'm not so hard on myself anymore. You can only do so much. I used to stay up cooking all night because I thought we had to have everything for every show. Now, if it's not there, it's just not there. I'm not so obsessed about what has to be done."

Since Sherrie recovered, she and Hugh have made the decision to keep their business small. They don't plan to move out of the house. Sherrie delegates more today. Her daughter Lauree has taken over production of the products and handles shipments as well as some sales. Lauree and granddaughter, Jennapher, do many of the craft fairs.

Unexpected turns of events have changed the course of Jasmine & Bread. Whereas at one time Sherrie wanted to continue to grow Jasmine & Bread into a large company, today she is more interested in a quality of life that is not, by its nature, so obsessive.

"In order to grow a business you have to be able to give it your all. I just can't anymore. I have to sleep. I have to take care of my health," Sherrie said. "Hugh and I aren't the ones to take it to the next level. I know what my strengths are and what my limitations are. I feel good that I have been around so long. Most small businesses fall by the wayside by five years. We've been in business over twelve."

How Driven Are You?

When Sherrie and Hugh started Jasmine & Bread they were fueled by Sherrie's desire to prove herself in the business world. Her energy was endless. No task was too small or large for her. When she met a dead end, she just turned around. She took advantage of all that was handed to her. This is the kind of commitment needed to start a business. At every turning point, every decision to keep growing larger, a new commitment is necessary to fuel the engine.

How driven are you? How is your health? Do both you and your spouse want to put all your time and energy into the business? There is sacrifice in growing a business. It will demand much of your energy, creative thinking, and time. The problems are endless. There will be one crisis after another to meet. Sleep will become the time when your unconscious works on a dilemma that just wouldn't unravel during waking hours. Or your sleeping time will be replaced by thinking time. Growing a business may demand obsessive behavior.

When one partner wants to grow and the other to stay small

The maxim "There is no such thing as equal" holds true for a couple in business. One spouse may have more drive and desire than the other. It was Jonathan Rutstein from Bread & Chocolate who wanted his own business. His wife, Fran, supported him and is in business with him, but it is his dream that fueled it. Hugh urged Sherrie from the start to open Jasmine & Bread and prides himself on his title of "Supportive Husband." It is clear to Lynne

Andreen from Uncle Dave's that her goals are different from her husband's.

"I would be happy to have a small boutique business," she said. "Dave and I are different. He will keep growing and growing. He loves business and would live in it twenty-four hours a day. I want time to do other things. I have been forced to grow, and he has been forced to slow down."

Then there are the couples whose desire to grow the business matches each other's. Judy and Jim MacIsaac from Highland Sugarworks are both driven to make their business big and successful. It's the same with Jonathan Altman and Carol Berry from Putney Pasta.

How big do you want to grow your business? Do you both have the same desire? How are you going to compromise and support each other's dreams? Talk to each other. Make sure it is clear how much each of you is willing to sacrifice to the business. And whatever you think it will take in terms of time and energy, double it.

How long can you live without a profit?

Jim MacIsaac from Highland Sugarworks knew early in his working life that he wanted his own business. His ambition, discipline and drive are necessary attributes for successfully running a business. Once he found his niche in producing and selling maple syrup, his drive has carried him through. Judy is equally energetic. Her training in retail sales, from a chic store on Rodeo Drive in Los Angeles to a Banana Republic clothing store in Burlington, helped hone her skills in sales. Competition fuels them both. They are a couple equally committed to growing their business as large as possible.

"Jim is obsessed with making a profit," Judy said. "And he

Sautéed Chicken Breasts with Maple and Spices

Living so close to Montpelier, Judy can call the New England Culinary Institute for inspiration. This recipe is one of Chef Michel LeBorgne, Maitre Cuisinier de France (M.C.F.).

3 tablespoons Highland Sugarworks Maple Syrup

2 teaspoons soy sauce

2 teaspoons crushed coriander

3 tablespoons butter

1 medium onion, chopped fine

a pinch of saffron

2 tomatoes, peeled, seeded and chopped

2 skinless, boneless chicken breasts, lightly pounded

1 tablespoon red wine vinegar

salt to taste

pepper to taste

1. In a small, non-reactive bowl, combine Highland Sugarworks Maple Syrup, soy sauce, and crushed coriander. Set aside.

2. In a heavy skillet melt 1 tablespoon of butter over medium heat. Add onions and sauté until translucent, about 20 minutes. Add the pinch of saffron and the tomatoes. Simmer until almost dry, about 10 minutes. Set aside.

3. Heat a non-reactive pan, add 2 tablespoons butter and sauté chicken breasts, 3 minutes on each side. Add the maple mixture from above, reduce heat and cook for 2 additional minutes. Remove chicken from skillet and set aside.

4. Add the onion/tomato/saffron reduction and red wine vinegar to the skillet. Cook on medium heat to reduce liquid by half. Add salt and pepper to taste.

5. To serve, pool sauce on a plate, slice chicken breast attractively and arrange slices on top of the sauce.

Makes 2 servings

is very good at it. He has been profitable since his first year in business. He is as adept at fixing pipes as he is at reading a spreadsheet. A perfect combination. And I love the challenge of selling. I love to sell, love my company."

They have grown their company to the third-largest distributor of maple syrup in Vermont.

"And the number-two spot isn't too far ahead," Jim said.

Jim and Judy are equally driven to succeed. They are ready to work as long and as hard as it takes to keep growing their business. And it is paying off. They have moved to a larger location, where both production facilities and office are together.

"It's really good," said Judy. "The move has been unbelievable. We have increased productivity threefold. Our infrastructure is strong. We have hired a new production manager, more production personnel, a new office manager, and new bookkeeper. We rehabbed an old building, bought new equipment. We're really growing our business here. It's no joke. It's no fly-by-night thing. It's not for sale. We're growing, and our vision is ten years down the road."

The Decision to Expand

When Jonathan Altman and Carol Berry from Putney Pasta were deciding on whether to move to a new location, they did a lot of talking. Were they ready to make the commitment? It meant they would probably have to move out of Putney, the town that gave their business its name. They were committed to keeping their company in Vermont, but would have to hunt to find an appropriate commercial building. They didn't want to move too far away, because they wanted their employees to come with them.

Did they want to recommit the next part of their lives to growing their business? What size did they want to become?

Of course we went for it; that's why we're in business!

"When Jon and I started to discuss moving, we weren't sure we wanted to make the huge financial leap," said Carol. "One day I had a revelation. What did we have to lose? Our house was already tied to the business. It had been used as collateral. So, whether we borrowed an additional $100,000 for expansion, or $1,000,000 to move, the personal risk felt the same. My brother put it this way: 'If you borrow $100,000, the bank owns you. If you borrow $1,000,000, you own the bank.' Of course we wanted to keep growing. That's why we started the business!"

"It took two years in all to find the building, secure the financing, and move," said Carol.

"It was a Herculean effort," Jonathan said. "These were the two most stressful years of our business. We were running at full capacity, twenty-four hours a day at our plant and, in the meantime, spending hours a day on the new building.

"We needed to find a location that offered municipal water, municipal sewer, and capacity for three-phase power. That is not easy to find in Vermont. Towns called us from all over the state. But we were committed to staying as close to Putney as possible. The building in Chester is only twenty miles from Putney. We signed a purchase and sales agreement in November 1992, and the sellers signed their half in February 1993. Then the real work began.

"There was so much to be done, and so much we had never done before. Carol and I drew straws to see who would do the financing and who would be in charge of licenses and permits. Carol won financing."

"Boy, did I get the short end of the stick," Carol said. "I stayed up running projections night after night. I didn't know how much electricity would cost in the new building. I had never heated a 41,000-square-foot space!"

Jonathan continued, "By the time we sat down at the closing in October 1993, there were sixteen people representing six separate agencies: the bank, the Small Business Association (SBA), the Vermont Industrial Development Association (VIDA), a local development authority, a regional development authority, and the town of Chester, through which we had received a federal grant. For the closing alone, if we had laid the pages side to side, there would have been one and one half miles of photocopies.

"There were lots of surprises along the way. When we first saw the building, it was fall. We went that winter to look and saw a few puddles inside. By spring it was clear that there would have to be a new roof. We renegotiated with the owner. We hired an architect, told him our budget, and he came in at double the amount. Carol stayed home for two days and designed the building. That's the plan we used. Construction was supposed to end in January. In midstream we changed from Freon refrigeration to ammonia refrigeration. We didn't move into the new building until June 1994.

"Then it took almost a year to get the kinks out of the system. We went from 4,000 square feet to 40,000 square feet; and from eighteen employees to forty.

"Our business has increased 100 percent and we have been profitable all along. We're very pleased.

"Between us things haven't changed much. As a couple you just deal with the stress. At the beginning there are smaller issues, then there are bigger issues, but you just deal with the issue. It's not about us, it's the situation. We've learned how we deal with an issue together. How each one deals with it. If it's an issue that doesn't have to get dealt with immediately, once you get home, that's when it gets addressed."

"We wanted to maintain, but to maintain is to grow"

Eric and Francine Chittenden from Cold Hollow Cider Mill have seen a lot of change in the business climate in the twenty-two years they have been in business. When they first bought the barn on Route 100 there was no such thing as zoning. They did not need permits to build. They saw what needed to be done and just did it. Today Eric finds himself constantly talking with officials about zoning, permits, and expenses.

"Doing business today is not as fun as it used to be," Eric said. "There is so much more bureaucracy. We never even had a business plan. We had the bad habit of spending all of our money and then going to the bank to ask for more, and they gave us the money.

"There is so much more expectation of a small business today. Everything is so profit driven. On a dairy farm every cow is an individual profit center and has her own chart. If Bessie eats more grain than she produces milk, Bessie is dog meat. It's like that with every product on every shelf. It's all the bottom line.

"And there are not the profits there used to be. Once anyone could open a business. Say, from a hobby. If you worked hard enough you'd be a success story. Today, you have to already have your wealth before you open."

Eric and Francine were considering franchising their business.

But around their fifteenth year in business they decided to stop expanding in order to stabilize. What they discovered was that there is no such thing as stabilizing a business.

"Expenses increase, profit margins decrease, so you might be selling the same amount of product but making less money. The outside community does not always see this. Employees do not always see this. We have to sell over $100,000 of product just to cover health insurance. But you can't stay still in a business," said Eric.

Whatever size business you and your spouse decide to grow, make it fit your lifestyle and your dreams. One reason to be in business is to have control over your destiny. Try to act rather than react to the momentum of your business. A business is always changing. Count on it.

9

Business as a
Way of Life

Growing, maintaining, and running a business will change
the way you live. Personal life often evolves from the needs
of the business. Conversation tends to circle around shop talk.
There will be times when you may think that all you do is work.
How do you combine work and family? Relationship and work?
Leisure time and work? How can a couple seek, find, and keep
balance in their lives? How do they juggle family, work, relationships, and civic responsibilities? How do these couples do it?

The immense learning curve that a couple will climb for the
first few years of their business will keep them absorbed and exhausted. Once the business has a structure and the systems are in
place, the job changes. The energies used to create an entity will
need to be channeled into running the business.

There will be constant challenges. The business outgrows its
space. One spouse may get sick. A product that used to be the
best-seller goes flat. A key employee will leave. Expensive ma-

---

Profile of Business Growth

Stage 1—Develop

　Growing customer base one at a time

　More money going into business than coming out

　Management focusing on finding customers, making products and paying vendors

　Tasks performed by any able body

　More work to do than hours in a day

Stage 2—Grow

　Break even

　Repeat customers

　Vendors secured

　Management focusing on marketing and sales

Stage 3—Maintain

　Sales consistent

　Ways of running business established

　Management focused on internal efficiency

　Hiring and training staff more specific to task

Stage 4—Expand

　Profits increasing each year

　Internal tasks well established and run by trained staff

　Focus of management on increasing profit by increasing production and efficiency

---

chinery will need to be replaced. Situations will present themselves constantly. That is part of running a business.

Ultimately, a business is always in a state of change: change that is outside the control of the couple. Each of these couples had a dream when they opened their business. What happens in reality can be quite different. As Davis Koier said, "Business constantly redefines itself. We try not to lose sight of the dream. Do we define our business, or do our customers define our business?"

How to Find Relief from Business Stress

Davis Koier from Ward's Pond Farm is facing different challenges in the eighth year of business than those in his first, second, or third.

"Our mail order is up, our wholesale is up, but the shows that we have relied on for cash flow are down as much as 50 percent from last year. There are more food people out there who have perceived shows as a cash-flow problem solver. The pie is divided into smaller wedges, and the economy in general is down. On the one hand we feel optimistic about our business in the areas where we can show gains. On the other hand, the day-to-day cash flow is a big problem. What it requires of us is to focus more on wholesale and mail-order business. We have to redefine ourselves. And anytime you make a switch in focus there is a need for new capital."

Not only does Davis have to change the focus of Ward's Pond Farm, he also is doing so without Ellen's full-time involvement. She is working full-time teaching, and their two children are in school. Ellen tries to keep up but finds that the business has a lower priority for her now than when they first started and before they had children.

When Ellen and Davis first opened Ward's Pond Farm everything was an adventure. Where they are now is much more a matter of survival. The stakes are different. There are employees and investors counting on Ward's Pond Farm to survive and thrive.

Davis finds relief from the business at home with his wife and children.

"We have found that business as a way of life has to be put on a different shelf than life as a way of life. There has to be a separation," said Davis. "There needs to be a point when you say to yourself, 'Yeah, yeah, I have all these worries and concerns, that's true. But I've got a wife and children and they have their needs, too.' I find a great deal of relief from the pressure of business by paying attention to them. That is a saving grace. It is interesting to me to see that the more pressure there is on me from the business, the more I tend to appreciate the moments I have with my children and my personal life."

Family has become a source of relief for Davis: a true measure of balance against the constant pressure of worry caused by running a small business.

Jonathan Rutstein from Bread & Chocolate finds balance in the small moments of life.

"Running a small business and having a life outside of it are practically impossible. When you don't have a lot of employees and you are essential to the day-to-day running of the business it is very difficult to separate from it. It's like a child. And children do funny things. You have to put so much time into it because it is so difficult and so changeable. I like January, February, and March because I go to watch my son play basketball twice a week. And that is good.

"I haven't found the key to how to separate myself totally from business. But I have been teaching a course at Linden State College, and I find that fun. Last year I taught entrepreneurship, and this year I am teaching marketing. After eight years in business it is fun to put all I have learned in some kind of order and talk to someone else about business instead of myself all of the time."

Is It Possible to Separate
Business and Life?

When completely immersed in the job of running a business, it can be hard to turn away from it to do other things. Every couple is different and has different needs. Richard and Diane Copley from The Herb Patch have the added constriction of having their business just outside their back door.

"In our case, our business is ten feet away and we have the business line ring into our house. Early on we used to get calls in the middle of the night. We used to panic. Often it was someone in a different time zone requesting information. We unplug it now. We refer to the business as The Herb Patch when we speak of it. But I would say in our case it is very hard to separate."

Richard stills leaves for what he calls his "day job," as freelance cameraman for NBC. Diane is *never* far away from the business.

"The bank likes to say 'Don't let Richard leave his day job.' But Diane wrestles with the finances constantly. It's a juggling act. I feel like we are always cash poor, always waiting for payment on an order. We're lending institutions ourselves, but we're not set up to be. I'd say we're trying to balance seven days a week."

Jonathan Altman, from Putney Pasta, recalls one of the first vacations they were able to take after opening their business. They were in Bermuda. It was a beautiful day. Carol and Jonathan were lying on the beach drinking piña coladas when a policeman approached them looking for Carol Berry. They raced to the telephone concerned about their son, Justin, but it was two employees from Putney Pasta calling for advice from Carol. Carol and Jonathan were relieved and at the same time questioned why they had to receive that phone call at all. It wasn't a life-or-death situation but it certainly put a temporary pall on their vacation.

"It's totally our life"

No qualms, no regret, no indecision, Judy and Jim MacIsaac from Highland Sugarworks have decided to build their business to the exclusion of all other activities—save their one-year-old son, Dylan.

"It's totally our life. Completely and totally," said Judy. "If I had to put it in perspective, I would say Dylan comes first, Highland Sugarworks second, and our marriage third. We waited four years to have a baby because Highland Sugarworks was our baby.

"The bottom line is that if you are going to do this craziness, husband and wife running a business together thing, you really have to stay focused on long-term goals. I try to separate my emotions from business. We don't cook anymore, we don't eat anymore. But we do provide for Dylan. One of us goes home from work at five or six to be with Dylan, and the other stays until nine or ten, and then we swap."

To relieve tension Judy and Jim follow the old axiom that change is as good as a rest, so they get up from their desks frequently to lend a hand in production. For both, it is a relief from the pressure.

> "There isn't a day that goes by without our saying, whether
> we're driving to work or sitting on the deck,
> 'God, aren't we lucky?' "
> —CAROL BERRY, Putney Pasta

Balance Is Relative

Starting and running a business requires an inordinate amount
of time and attention. There is a trade-off in any choice made in
life. When a couple chooses to open a business, the concessions
are often lack of free time, less time with family and friends, and
financial sacrifice. The couple's personal relationship is often sub-
ordinated to the needs of the business. This can be true for years.
Eric and Francine from Cold Hollow Cider Mill have sacrificed
a lot to grow their business. "I would have liked to travel more,"
said Francine. "Mostly we did what we did because we're stub-
born and really hate the idea of working for someone else or
admitting defeat. Most of what good fortune we've had has been
because we have a lot of perseverence and we choose really good
people to work with us.

"You can't live through something like being in business together for over twenty-one years and come out unscathed. A sense
of humor is definitely worth its weight in gold."

Are you willing to sacrifice other aspects of your life in order
to grow your business? Do you believe wholeheartedly in your
ability to persevere? Will you both be able to juggle home responsibilities with the demands of the business? Can you keep focused?

Although the hours are long and gratification delayed, the
rewards are there, albeit hard to see, when you're in the thick of
running a business. To create your own reality; to define who
you are as a person and a couple; to constantly be forced to find
solutions and overcome obstacles; to see in each other the growth
of confidence that happens when failure is surmounted and success is achieved builds strong people—in this case, couples—who
have a lot of knowledge and understand the meaning and value

of hard work. They are role models for their children, important contributors to their communities.

The satisfaction of responding to that first phone call, of selling the first big order, of finally breaking even, of greeting a customer, supplier, or distributor to talk about your business, of having the ability to hire employees, and of knowing that what you are doing is making a difference—are among the many rewards.

Mediterranean Ravioli Salad

A perfect salad for a summer's picnic or a Sunday brunch.

2 9-ounce packages Putney Pasta Spinach and Feta Ravioli

3 tablespoons olive oil plus oil for lightly coating cooked ravioli

6 cloves garlic, peeled and minced

1 1/2 cups broccoli florets, blanched

1 1/2 cups cauliflower florets, blanched

1 cup white beans, cooked

2 ounces sun-dried tomatoes, oil-packed, julienned

2 bunches arugula leaves

1 tablespoon Romano cheese, grated

coarse ground black pepper, to taste

1. Cook ravioli according to package directions, lightly oil and chill.

2. In a large skillet heat the 3 tablespoons of olive oil over medium heat. Add garlic and cook until lightly toasted. Add blanched broccoli and cauliflower, white beans and sun-dried tomatoes. Sauté for 3 to 4 minutes. Remove from heat.

3. In a large bowl toss vegetable mixture with cooked ravioli and arugula leaves.

4. Top with grated Romano cheese and ground black pepper.

5. Serve. (For variety add freshly grilled chicken or shrimp.)

Makes 6 to 8 servings

Conclusion

It's Not the Destination,
It's the Journey

Where are the ten couples on their journey of business?
Six of the businesses have been affected by a dip in sales caused by increased competition in the specialty food industry. To compensate, they have been forced to adapt. Some are considering selling. Jonathan and Fran from Bread & Chocolate are trying to find different ways to utilize their new building. Richard still works regularly as a cameraman while Diane holds down the shop at The Herb Patch. At Jasmine & Bread, Hugh and Sherrie are still cooking in their kitchen, and are contemplating selling. Ellen and Davis from Ward's Pond Farm are trying to increase their wholesale and mail-order departments. Lynne and Dave from Uncle Dave's are looking for the next big

deal. Marilyn and Harry are considering selling Yesterday's Kitchen.

Eric and Francine from Cold Hollow Cider Mill and Jacki and Ron from Mother Myrick's are where they always are, working in their businesses that feel like home and act like family while still selling quite a lot of product.

Judy and Jim from Highland Sugarworks are parenting Dylan while growing their business to the next level of success. Jonathan and Carol are fine-tuning their infrastructure at Putney Pasta, enjoying much growth.

What would these couples tell you if you asked them about going into business together?

They would want you to make sure that making a lot of money is not your only motivation. These couples made lifestyle choices, to live in a place they love and to be their own bosses.

Don't quit your day job. One of you must be willing to support the other unless you have saved enough money to finance the business and buy the groceries for twice as long as you think it will take to get established.

If you find that it isn't working, that your relationship is suffering, have an exit strategy. A successful couple doesn't always make a successful business partnership.

They all agree on this: It will never be boring and if you are looking for a challenge, you have found one.

These couples know about dreams and fulfilling them. They know about the hard work and compromise that is inevitable with any choice. They've experienced the stress that comes with risk, sharing power, and the responsibility of ownership. They are learning how to tolerate that stress and to forgive each other for being human. They're wise to their own and their partners' strengths and weaknesses. They know how to accept each other's decisions, sometimes even gracefully. They are experts at sacrifice, work on communication, know the healing power of laughter, cheer their own accomplishments, and depend on the commitment that they have made to their business.

Running a business is never easy. Running it with a spouse dissolves boundaries between family and work. A couple who work together will change their relationship. Romance may give way to work. The ready ear that was available before when each worked at different jobs no longer carries objectivity. Situations in the business that cause dissension may spill over into the relationship.

Each couple in this book has developed ways of communicating with each other that work. They have had to. It was the only way the business and relationship would survive.

All have benefited from the experience of creating a business together. They have all grown, individually, and as a couple. Some like it, some don't. Some will probably not be in business for much longer. Some will probably be running their creations for many years. But they are none the worse for the effort it takes to start, grow, and maintain a business. After all, business is what this society is made of.

So before you make the jump, consider seriously the downside of being in business together. Remember you are betting on a lot of important aspects of your life—your relationship, the security of your family, your financial situation, and your future. This is hard work. For all those who make it, there are many more who don't.

If after considering all the pluses and minuses of being in business together, it still seems like a great idea, and both of you are game—take the chance! Dig in and squirm a little in the fullness of knowing your spouse. Together you will create something bigger than either of you could do alone. And you'll never be able to say to each other, "If only we had tried . . ."

The Businesses

Fran and Jonathan Rutstein   1-802-429-2920
BREAD & CHOCOLATE, INC.   Fax: 1-802-429-2990
1 Cross Street
PO Box 305
Wells River, VT 05081-0305

Product Line: Chocolate Dessert Sauces, Instant Flavored Cocoas, Lemonades, White Cream Beverages, Lollipops

Francine and Eric Chittenden   1-800-327-7537(U.S.)
COLD HOLLOW CIDER MILL   1-800-3-APPLES(VT)
Rte. 100, Box 430
Waterbury Ctr., VT 05677

Product Line: Fruit Preserves, Apple Cider, Apple Cider Syrup Granola, Mustard, Mulling Spices, Apple Sauce

Diane and Richard Copley   1-802-235-2466
THE HERB PATCH, LTD.   Fax: 1-802-235-2470
Pawlet Road
PO Box 1111
Middletown Springs, VT 05757

Product Line: Salt-Free Culinary Blends, Herbal Teas, Vinegars, Chocolate, Seasonings, Flavored Cocoa and Honey

Judy and Jim MacIsaac   1-800-452-4012
HIGHLAND SUGARWORKS, INC.   Fax: 1-802-479-1737
PO Box 58
Websterville, VT 05678

Product Line: Maple Syrup and other Pure Maple Products, Pancake
Mix

Sherrie and Hugh Maurer   1-802-763-7115
JASMINE & BREAD, INC.   Fax: 1-802-237-1139
RR#2, Box 256
S. Royalton, VT 05068

Product Line: Beyond Catsup, Beyond Belief Salsa, Beyond
Horseradish, Mustard, Horseradish Jelly, BBQ Sauce, Marinara Sauce

Jacki Baker and Ron Mancini   1-802-362-1560
MOTHER MYRICK'S   Fax: 1-802-362-1721
CONFECTIONERY
PO Box 1142
Rte. 7A
Manchester, VT 05255

Product Line: Handmade Confections, Executive Gift Mail-Order
Service

Carol Berry and Jonathan Altman   1-802-875-4500
PUTNEY PASTA COMPANY, INC.   Fax: 1-802-875-3322
PO 445
Chester, VT 05143-0445

Product Line: Gourmet Vegetarian Pastas and Sauces

Lynne Andreen and David Lyon   1-802-824-3600
UNCLE DAVE'S KITCHEN, INC.   Fax: 1-802-824-6033
PO Box 2034, Rte. 100
S. Londonderry, VT 05155

Product Line: Condiments, Pasta sauces, Snack Foods, Seasonings

Ellen and Davis Koier   1-802-888-3001
WARD'S POND FARM, INC.   Fax: 1-802-888-3018
RFD #3, Box 1380
Morrisville, VT 05661

Product Line: Maple Roasted Almonds, Cashews, and Pecans; Smoked Almonds, Pecans, and Cashews; Smoked Onions, Vinegars in Ceramic Containers

Marilyn Wedig and Harry Haff
YESTERDAY'S KITCHEN, INC.

In the fall of 1996, Yesterday's Kitchen closed due to personal and family circumstances.

Appendix: Sources and Resources

Small Business Administration (SBA)

"The fundamental purposes of the Small Business Administration are to aid, counsel, assist, and protect the interests of small business; ensure that the small business concerns receive a fair portion of Government purchases, contracts, and subcontracts, as well as the sales of Government property; make loans to small business concerns, State and local development companies, and the victims of floods or other catastrophes, or of certain types of economic injury; and license, regulate, and make loans to small business investment companies."

Small Business Administration
409 Third Street SW
Washington, DC 20416
1-800-U-ASK-SBA

Hundreds of pamphlets are available from SBA concerning all aspects of running a business. Write to:

SBA
P.O. Box 15434
Fort Worth, Texas 76119

Field Offices—Small Business Administration
Taken from: U.S. Government Manual, July 1, 1995

Region 1

Boston, MA	9th Fl., 155 Federal St., 02110	617-451-2020
Augusta, ME	Rm. 512, 40 Western Ave., 04330	207-622-8378
Concord, NH	Suite 202, 143 N. Main St., 03302-1257	603-255-1400
Hartford, CT	2d Fl., 330 Main St., 06106	203-240-4700
Montpelier, VT	Rm. 205, 87 State St., 05602	802-828-4422
Providence, RI	5th Fl., 380 Westminister Mall, 02903	401-528-4561
Springfield, MA	Rm. 212, 1550 Main St., 01103	413-785-0268

Region 2

New York, NY	Rm 31-08, 26 Federal Plz., 10278	212-264-0750
Buffalo, NY	Rm. 1311, 111 W. Huron St., 14202	716-846-4301
Elmira, NY	4th Fl., 333 E. Water St., 14901	607-734-8130

Hato Rey, PR	Rm. 691, Federal Bldg., Carlos Chardon Ave.	809-766-5572
Melville, NY	Rm. 102E., 35 Pinelawn Rd., 11747	516-454-0750
Newark, NJ	4th Fl., 60 Park Pl., 07102	201-645-2434
Rochester, NY	Rm. 410, 100 State St., 14614	716-363-6700
Albany, NY	Rm. 815, Clinton and Pearl St., 12207	518-472-6300
Camden, NJ	2600 Mt. Ephraim Ave., 08104	609-757-5183
St. Croix, VI	Suite 7, 4200 United States Shopping Plz., 00820-4487	809-778-5380
St. Thomas, VI	Rm 210, Federal Office Bldg.,Veterans Dr., 00802	809-774-8530
Syracuse, NY	Rm 1071, 100 S. Clinton St., 13260	315-423-5383

Region 3

Philadelphia, PA	Suite 201, Allendale Sq., 475 Allendale Rd., King of Prussia, 19406	215-962-3710
Baltimore, MD	3d Fl., 10 N. Calvert St., 21202	410-962-4392
Clarksburg, WV	5th Fl., 168 West Main St., 26301	304-623-5631
Pittsburgh, PA	5th Fl., 960 Penn Ave., 15222	412-644-2780

Richmond, VA	Rm. 3015, 400 N.E. St., 23240	804-771-2400
Washington, DC	1110 Vermont Ave., NW., 20036	202-606-4000
Charleston, WV	Rm. 309, 550 Eagan St., 25301	304-347-5220
Harrisburg, PA	Rm 309, 100 Chestnut St., 17101	717-782-3840
Wilkes-Barre, PA	Rm. 2327, 20 N. Pennsylvania Ave., 18702	717-826-6497
Wilmington, DE	Suite 412, 920 N. King St., 19801	302-573-6295

Region 4

Altanta, GA	6th Fl.,1720 Peachtree St., NE, 30367-8102	404-347-4749
Birmingham, AL	Suite 200, 2121 8th Ave. N., 35202-2398	205-731-1344
Charlotte, NC	Suite A2015, 200 N. College St., 28202-2137	704-344-6563
Columbia, SC	Rm. 358, 1835 Assembly St., 29201	803-765-5376
Coral Gables, FL	Suite 501, 1320 Dixie Hwy., 33146-2911	305-536-5521
Jackson, MS	Suite 400, 101 W. Capitol St., 39201	601-965-4378
Jacksonville, FL	Suite 100-B, 7825 Baymeadows Way, 32256-7504	904-443-1900
Louisville, KY	Rm. 188, 600 Dr. M. L. King, Jr., Pl., 40202	502-582-5971

Nashville, TN	Suite 201, 50 Vantage Way, 37228-1500	615-736-5881
Gulfport, MS	Suite 1001, 1 Hancock Plz., 39501-7758	601-863-4449
Statesboro, GA	Rm. 225, 52 N. Main St., 30458	912-489-8719
Tampa, FL	Suite 104, 501 E. Polk St., 33602-3945	813-228-2594
West Palm Beach, FL	Suite 402, 5601 Corporate Way, 33407-2044	407-689-3922

Region 5

Chicago, IL	Rm. 1250, 500 W. Madison St., 60661-2511	312-353-4528
Cincinnati, OH	Suite 870, 525 Vine St., 45202	513-684-2814
Cleveland, OH	Suite 630, 1111 Superior Ave., 44199	216-522-4180
Columbus, OH	Suite 1400, 2 Nationwide Plz., 43215-2592	614-469-6860
Detroit, MI	Rm. 515, 477 Michigan Ave., 48226	313-226-6075
Indianapolis, IN	Suite 100, 429 N. Pennsylvania, 46204-1873	317-226-7272
Madison, WI	Rm. 213, 212 E. Washington Ave., 53703	608-264-5261
Minneapolis, MN	Suite 610, 100 N. 6th St., 55403-1563	612-370-2324
Marquette, MN	300 S. Front St., 49885	906-225-1108

Milwaukee, WI	Suite 400, 310 W. Wisconsin Ave., 53203	414-297-3941
Springfield, IL	Suite 302, 511 W. Capital St., 62704	217-492-4416

Region 6

Dallas, TX	Bldg. C, 8625 King George Dr., 75235-3391	214-767-7611
Albuquerque, NM	Suite 320, 625 Silver Ave., S.W., 87102	505-766-1870
Dallas, TX	Suite 114, 4300 Amon Carter Blvd., 76155	817-885-6500
El Paso, TX	Suite 320, 10737 Gateway West., 79935	915-540-5676
Harlingen, TX	Rm. 500, 222 E. Van Buren St., 78550	512-427-8533
Houston, TX	Suite 550, 9301 Southwestern Fwy., 77074-1591	713-773-6500
Little Rock, AR	Suite 100, 2120 Riverfront Dr., 72202	501-324-5278
Lubbock, TX	Suite 200, 1611 10th St., 79401	806-743-7462
New Orleans, LA	Suite 2000, 1661 Canal St., 70112	504-589-6685
Oklahoma City, OK	Suite 670, 200 N.W. 5th St., 73102	405-231-4301
San Antonio, TX	Suite 200, 7400 Blanco Rd., 78216	210-229-4535
Corpus Christi, TX	Suite 1200, 606 N. Carancahus, 78476	512-888-3331

Fort Worth, TX	Rm 8A-27, 819 Taylor St., 76102	817-334-3777
Austin, TX	Rm 520, 300 E. 8th St., 78701	512-482-5288
Marshall, TX	Rm 103, 505 E. Travis, 75670	903-935-5257
Shreveport, LA	Rm 8A-08, 500 Fannin St., 71101	318-676-3196

Region 7

Kansas City, MO	13th Fl., 911 Walnut St., 64106	816-426-3316
Cedar Rapids, IO	Suite 100, 373 Collins Rd. N.E., 52402-3147	319-393-8630
Des Moines, IA	Rm. 749, 210 Walnut St., 50309	515-284-4422
Kansas City, MO	Suite 501, 323 W. 8th St., 64105	816-374-6708
Omaha, NE	11145 Mill Valley Rd., 68154	402-221-4691
St. Louis, MO	Rm. 242, 815 Olive St., 63101	314-539-6600
Wichita, KS	Suite 510, 100 E. English St., 67202	316-269-6237
Springfield, MO	Suite 110, 620 S. Glenstone St., 65802-3200	417-864-7670

Region 8

Denver, CO	7th Fl., North Twr., 633 17th St., 80202-3607	303-294-7022
Casper, WY	Rm. 4001, 100 East B St., 82602-2839	307-261-5761

Fargo, ND	Rm. 218, 657 2d Ave. N., 58108-3086	701-239-5131
Helena, MT	Rm. 528, 301 S. Park, 59626	406-449-5381
Salt Lake City, UT	Rm. 2237, 125 S. State St., 84138-1195	801-524-5804
Sioux Falls, SD	Suite 101, 101 S. Main Ave., 57102-0527	605-330-4231

Region 9

Fresno, CA	Suite 107, 2719 N. Air Fresno Dr., 93727-1547	209-487-5189
Glendale, CA	Suite 1200, 330 N. Brand Blvd., 91203-2304	213-894-2956
Honolulu, HI	Rm. 2213, 300 Ala Moana Blvd., 96850-1025	808-541-2990
Las Vegas, NV	Rm. 301, 301 E. Stewart St., 89125-2527	702-388-6611
Phoenix, AZ	Suite 800, 2828 N. Central Ave., 85004-1025	602-640-2316
San Diego, CA	Suite 4-S-29, 880 Front St., 92188-0270	619-557-7252
San Francisco, CA	4th Fl., 211 Main St., 94105-1988	415-744-6820
Santa Ana, CA	Suite 160, 901 W. Civic Center Dr.	714-836-2494
Agana, GU	Rm. 508, 238 Archbishop F. C. Flores St., 96910	671-472-7277

Sacramento, CA	Rm. 215, 660 J St.,	
	95814-2413	916-551-1426
Reno, NV	Rm. 238, 50 S. Virginia	
	St., 89505-3216	702-784-5268
Tucson, AZ	Rm. 7-H, 300 W. Con-	
	gress St., 85701-1319	602-670-4759
Ventura, CA	Suite 10, 6477 Tele-	
	phone Rd., 93003-4459	805-642-1866

Region 10

Anchorage, AK	Rm. 67, 222 W. 8th	
	Ave., 99513-7559	907-271-4022
Boise, ID	Suite 290, 1020 Main	
	St., 83702-5754	208-334-1696
Portland, OR	Suite 500, 222 S.W. Co-	
	lumbia, 97201-6605	503-326-2682
Seattle, WA	Rm. 1792, 915 2d Ave.,	
	98174-1088	206-220-6520
Spokane, WA	10th Fl. E., W. 601 1st	
	Ave., 99204-0317	509-353-2800

Small Business Development Centers (SBDC)—Provides counseling and training to existing and potential small-business owners. These services are available at approximately 750 geographically dispersed locations.

Office of Small Business Development Centers
1-202-205-6766

Service Corps of Retired Executives (SCORE)—an organization of businesspeople available for assistance in business start-up.

409 3rd Street SW
Suite 5900
Washington, DC 20024
1-202-6762

Computer Software for Employee Manual
The Employee Manual Maker

Company: Jian
1975 W. El Camino Real
Suite 301
Mountain View, CA 94040-2218
Fax: 415-254-5640

Further Reading on Couples in Business

Barnett, Frank and Sharan. *Working Together, Entrepreneurial Couples.* Ten Speed Press, 1988.
Jaffee, Dennis T., Ph.D. *Working with the Ones You Love, Strategies for a Successful Family Business.* Conari Press, 1991.
O'Shea-Roch, Annette, and Malmberg, Sieglinde. *Partners at Home and at Work.* Self-Counsel Press, 1994.